NOTES OF TRAVEL
through the territory
of ARIZONA

NOTES O

NOTES OF TRAVEL

THROUGH THE

TERRITORY OF ARIZONA;

BEING

AN ACCOUNT OF THE TRIP

MADE BY

GENERAL GEORGE STONEMAN AND OTHERS

IN THE

AUTUMN OF 1870.

BY J. H. MARION.

PRESCOTT,
OFFICE OF THE ARIZONA MINER
1870

RAVEL THROUGH THE TERRITORY OF ARIZONA

Being an account of the trip made by
General George Stoneman and others
in the Autumn of 1870

By J. H. MARION
Edited by DONALD M. POWELL

THE UNIVERSITY OF ARIZONA PRESS / TUCSON / 1965

The University of Arizona Press
www.uapress.arizona.edu

Printed in the United States of America
21 20 19 18 17 16   7 6 5 4 3 2

ISBN-13: 978-0-8165-0068-0 (cloth)
ISBN-13: 978-0-8165-3532-3 (Century Collection paper)

Reproductions of the original cover and text page courtesy Denver
Public Library Western Collection.

L. C. Catalog Card No. 65-25160

♾ This paper meets the requirements of ANSI/NISO Z39.48-1992
(Permanence of Paper).

NOTES OF TRAVEL
through the territory
of ARIZONA

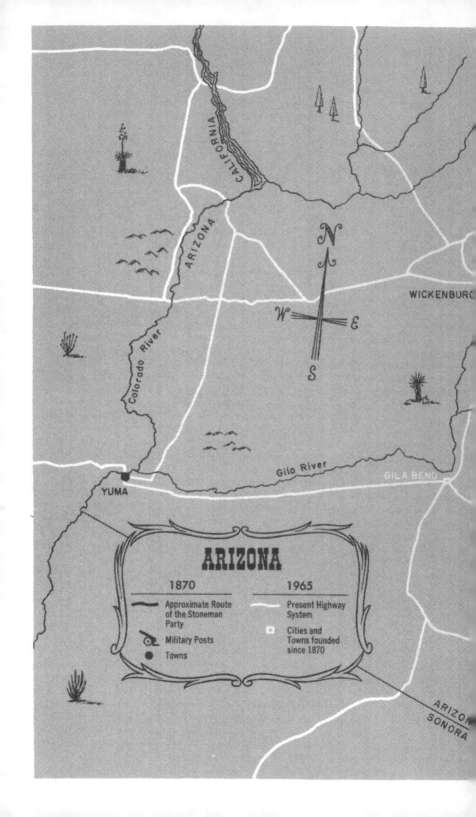

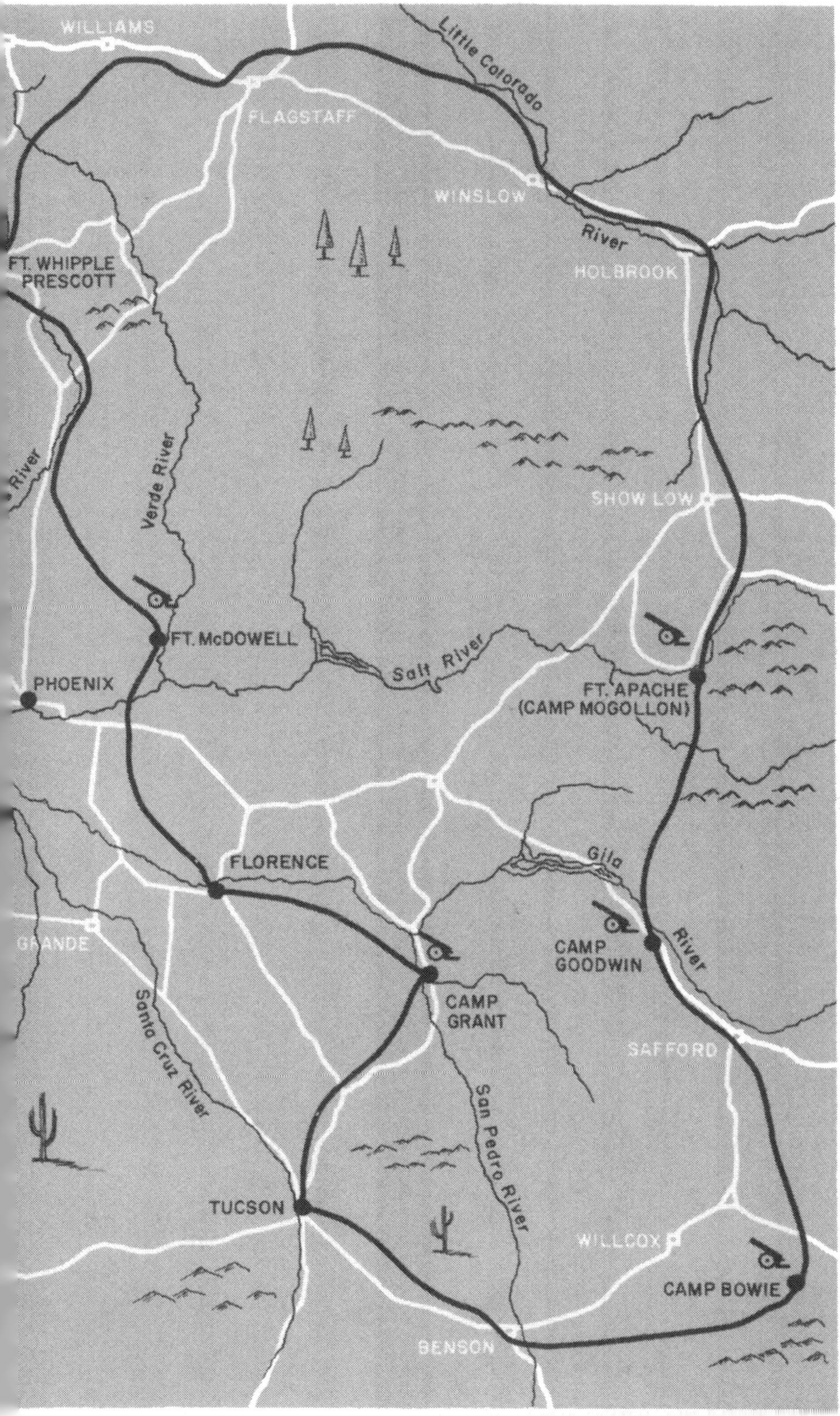

WILLIAMS
Little Colorado
FLAGSTAFF
WINSLOW
River
HOLBROOK
FT. WHIPPLE
PRESCOTT
Verde River
River
SHOW LOW
FT. McDOWELL
PHOENIX
Salt River
FT. APACHE
(CAMP MOGOLLON)
FLORENCE
Gila
River
CAMP
GOODWIN
GRANDE
Santa Cruz River
CAMP
GRANT
SAFFORD
San Pedro River
TUCSON
WILLCOX
CAMP BOWIE
BENSON

Of all the frontier editors, John Marion was the most forthright, had the greatest exuberance of expression and was the most fearless champion of causes lost or lagging that Arizona of the sixties and seventies produced. His columns swing the reader with a bang right into a live personality . . . . His incisive articles on the Indian question were notable. Clear in his convictions and bold in his expression of them, he was a man suited to the dangerous times in which he lived.

Thus writes Estelle Lutrell in "Arizona's Frontier Press," and it would be hard to say it better.[1]

---

[1]*Arizona Historical Review*, vol. 6, p. 21, Jan. 1935.

AN INTRODUCTION
by Donald M. Powell

JOHN HUGUENOT MARION was born in Louisiana, possibly in
New Orleans, in 1836 or 1837. If he knew he did not say.
"When a mere boy" he moved with his family to St. Louis
where he grew up. In 1853 or 1854, the *Courier* records, he
went to California and settled at Oroville. There he learned
the printing trade. He worked also at Marysville but must
have returned to St. Louis because in 1856 and 1857 he was
employed by the *Republican*.[2] This must have finished his
education as a newspaperman, for when he began publishing
the *Miner* in 1867 his journalistic style was fully formed.

When Marion returned to California we do not know,
but in the *Courier* of February 23, 1884 he says he "left San
Francisco the 6th day of October, 1863 on the brig Hidalgo"
for the sun-kissed land and had been there ever since. His
first stop was Yuma where he did some mining — unspeci-
fied — in 1864. Records in the Masonic Lodge in Prescott
show that Marion arrived there in 1864, the year of its found-
ing, with the Boggs and Will Short party.

He did not at once practice his trade. The tiny, raw
capital in the pine hills buzzed with the excitement of the
placer gold discoveries along Lynx Creek, the Agua Fria, the

2*Courier*, May 12, 1887.

Hassayampa, and elsewhere. Marion already had the fever, as did most young men of the time, and the cool, pure mountain air did not lower it. For several years he prospected and mined in various locations, apparently making a go of it but never striking it rich. On July 13 of 1866 he left Prescott with a party of thirty-nine men which called itself the "White Mountain Prospecting and Exploring Company." They were gone three months crossing the Mogollon Plateau and exploring the White Mountains, going as far north as the Zuñi villages. Then they turned south through western New Mexico and into the Gila Valley, then west along the Gila, and eventually northwest across the mountains to the Verde Valley and Prescott which they reached on October 17.[3]

There was no gold, and in Marion's opinion there was little prospect of finding any in the country over which they passed. As for silver, he said later, the old prospectors knew very little about it and cared less. As an example he recalled that he and former Prescott Mayor William Kelly camped, while on prospect, near the famous Peck mine, broke rock on it, and did not realize that it was loaded with silver. The mine later yielded over a million in less than two years.

Perhaps it was this experience that finally convinced Marion that the pen was mightier than the pick. In any event later in the year 1867 he purchased the *Miner,* a paper which had been started at Whipple in 1864, printed on a press brought from Santa Fe by Territorial secretary Richard McCormick and hauled to its destination with the party which organized the Territorial government. He brought out his first issue on September 21.[4]

From then to the abrupt end of his life Marion was Prescott's best known newspaper man. Until 1877 he was editor

---

[3] In the *Miner* for January 26, 1867 Marion published a diary of the trip. Most of the country they saw was unsettled forest and mountain. This diary is less interesting than his account of his journey with Stoneman.

[4] Estelle Lutrell. "Arizona's Frontier Press," *Arizona Historical Review.* vol. 6, pp. 9–10, Jan. 1935.

and part owner of the *Miner*, Marion's *Miner* it was affectionately called. Then, briefly, he published the *Arizonian* and the *Enterprise*. As has been remarked he was always buying and selling off bits of his papers. In 1882 he established the *Morning Courier* which is still published today.[5]

Marion was a life-long Democrat and his editorials laid blame for most of the Territory's lack of progress at the door of the Republican party. In the manner of the day he wielded his pen sometimes like a rapier, sometimes like a bludgeon. Right or wrong, he was never dull, and he was widely beloved and admired. He was always a booster for Arizona whose beauty he admired extravagantly and a booster of his beloved Prescott, surely the finest place to live this side of Paradise. There are a number who still agree with him.

His stand on the Indian question was plain. Arizona would never prosper until the Indians were banished from its fertile valleys and mesas so that the land was safe for whites. It was a point of view with which most of his western contemporaries thoroughly agreed. The Apaches should be hunted down, severly chastised, and then herded on reservations where it would be the duty of the federal government to keep them, and then, if possible — there were doubts — to civilize them. Writing in the *Miner* for June 4, 1870, he deplored the policy of feasting the Indian "at the public crib." It had never worked; it never would. He cited what had happened to settlers along the Verde and the Salt. The policy had been pursued at Goodwin with the same results. The Indians "would one day talk peace and gorge themselves out of the commissary, and the next, inbrue their hands in the blood of some white man, rob a ranch, or stampede a Government herd." There was, he continued, plenty of room in the West for everyone, and if the Indian was only disposed to let the settler alone, all would be well.

---

[5]Details of his ownership and editorship will be found in Estelle Lutrell's *Newspapers and Periodicals of Arizona, 1859–1911*, and in the Centennial edition of the *Courier*, May 15, 1964.

"Now, this Territory was acquired by the blood and treasure of white men, and we contend that white men have as much right to exist upon its soil as have the savages. And, recollect, they have nothing of which we care to dispossess them. The land is not theirs, but it was purchased from Mexico and thrown open to settlement by our Government. This being the case we are at a loss to account for the absurd sayings and doings of those people of our own race who side with the Savages and accuse us of robbing, cheating, and swindling them."

The Indian, Marion concluded, was better off than he ever had been and would become better off if he would settle down and make himself useful. But there was little hope of that. ". . . not until they are whipped into submission and taught that white men — American citizens — have rights which they are bound to respect. . . . It is about time the Government set about it in earnest by sending more regular troops here and making vigorous, persistent war upon them, or, by raising sufficient force of volunteers to accomplish that much desired result."

When General George Stoneman in command of the newly created army Department of Arizona arrived in Prescott in July of 1870 Marion welcomed him as the saviour of Arizona who would deal sternly with Apaches and free the settlers from constant dread of fire, mutilation and death.

Stoneman, an army officer with a fine reputation, was no neophyte in the Southwest. He had been born in Chatauqua County, New York, in August 1822, and, according to a brief autobiographical statement he wrote about 1888, now in the Bancroft Library, he learned surveying at the age of seventeen with the idea of going West. When he was eighteen he read a story in the *Southern Literary Messenger* laid at West Point. Inspired, he applied for an appointment and was admitted.[6]

---

[6]Stoneman's memory appears to have been faulty. I have not located such a story in the *Messenger* for the period.

Upon graduation Lieutenant Stoneman was assigned to the First Regiment, U.S. Dragoons, Company "C," at Fort Leavenworth. When he arrived he found his company had already left with Kearny's Army of the West for California, and he was detailed to conduct an ammunition train west. From Santa Fe he continued west as assistant quartermaster to the Mormon Battalion. In 1853 he escorted a survey party from Benicia, California, to San Antonio, Texas. Before the Civil War he had crossed southern Arizona twice.

Stoneman was mustered out of the service at the close of the Civil War as major general of volunteers, and on reorganization of the army he was promoted to permanent rank of colonel of the Twenty First Regular Infantry and brevet major general in the regular army. It is this difference between regular and brevet (temporary) rank which causes confusion in accounts of the period when officers are sometimes addressed by their regular rank and sometimes by their higher, or brevet, rank.

One of Stoneman's first actions in Arizona was to visit Camp Verde in the heart of the Apache country. This he did in late July, 1870, and he was accompanied by John Marion and several other citizens of Prescott. The general and the young newspaper publisher must have become friends, for when Stoneman left Prescott in late August for an extended swing around the chief military installations of Arizona, Marion accompanied him.

Marion's account of his trip with Stoneman, one of the best and least known such accounts from this period, appeared in the *Miner* in installments between October 8 and November 19, 1870. It was so widely read that he announced in the *Miner* of December 24 that seven hundred copies had been printed and were for sale at the *Miner* office for fifty cents. Only three appear to have survived.[7] It speaks for itself in the following pages.

---

[7]Copies are in the Huntington Library, San Marino, California, in the library at Yale University and in the Western Collection of the Denver Public Library.

No suitable quarters were available at Fort Whipple, and Stoneman spent the winter at Drum Barracks in California, a move for which he was widely criticized in Arizona, and he only returned to the headquarters of his command briefly in the following spring. His own report prepared following his trip of inspection is dated October 31, 1870, but it was not immediately available; at least rumors of its content did not reach Arizona for several months.

The report was finally published in the Tucson *Citizen* on April 15, 1871 and in the *Miner* on May 6. Immediately a storm of denunciation from all over Arizona broke over the general's head. Of the fifteen military posts in the Territory, Stoneman recommended that seven be abandoned including Whipple, Lowell, McDowell, and Crittenden. Of the three quartermaster depots all except Yuma should be broken up and the civilian employees discharged. There would remain, in order of importance named, Verde, Thomas, Grant (to be relocated) and Bowie, Date Creek, Mojave, and Yuma. Rigid economy was recommended at the remaining posts, and the general spent some time complaining of the high prices charged the army for freight, and for defective and sub-standard goods. Only in the final paragraphs did he "reluctantly" touch on the Apache problem, and of that he concluded, ". . . . since the organization of the department, the Hualapais, Apaches, Mojaves or Yavapais, and the Coyotero Apaches have become quiet and are fast becoming domesticated. Cachies[8] . . . has expressed a wish to go on a reservation." Only the Pinals and Tontos were openly hostile, but the Apache nation as a whole was nearly harmless as compared with twenty years earlier.

Despite the fact that most of Stoneman's criticisms of exorbitant prices for supplies and shoddy materials were true and that abandonment of several of the smaller posts was sound, it is apparent that many of his judgements were ill-

---

[8] i.e., Cochise.

considered, based on insufficient knowledge of the situation in Arizona, and certainly ill-timed. The freighters whose supply trains were attacked, plundered, and burned did not consider that the Apaches were quiet and rapidly becoming domesticated. The central Arizona settlers whose ranches were attacked and burned, whose stock was driven off and killed did not consider that the Apaches were nearly harmless. The town merchants, of course, argued that they were only making fair return for the risks they undertook.

The Tucson newspapers first got wind of Stoneman's report and opened the chorus of furious indignation that greeted it everywhere. Lowell be abandoned, indeed. Marion in the *Miner* first urged moderation and caution pending receipt of the full text, but finally in the same issue in which it was printed in full he was forced to write, "Since the organization of the Territory, in 1863, no act of any military officer has so unnerved the hearts of the brave settlers of Arizona as this same report of Col. George Stoneman." Its statements were "astounding and sickening."

The Territorial legislature then meeting in Tucson immediately began collecting evidence to refute Stoneman's conclusions on the peaceful tendencies of the Apaches. This resulted in the publication of a rare pamphlet of *Memorials and Affidavits Showing Outrages Perpetrated by the Apache Indians, in the Territory of Arizona, During the Years 1869 and 1870*, published in San Francisco in 1871, thirty-two pages of testimony to raids, ambushes, robberies, and murder, some of which went on at the time Stoneman was touring the pacified area.

That same spring, perhaps convinced that the military would make no determined effort against the Indians, a group of Tucson citizens and Papagos from the nearby reservation on April 30 made a dawn attack on a camp of Apaches living near Camp Grant and killed about one hundred twenty men, women and children in what has become known as the Camp Grant Massacre. It was deplored in the East, but was wholeheartedly approved in Arizona.

Justified or not in his criticism, Stoneman's usefulness in Arizona was at an end even though Marion urged his readers not to blame the Colonel too much, "for, with exceptions, he has done his duty by the territory." The same issue carried the news that General George Crook had been named to command the Department of Arizona.

That same year, 1871, Stoneman was placed on the retired list and settled on a ranch in the San Gabriel Valley in California. The following year he was appointed Railroad Commissioner of California and was elected to the same office at the next general election. In 1882 he was elected governor of California. He served capably and declined renomination in 1886. He died in 1894.

Through his newspapers Marion continued to be the voice of central Arizona, demanding a solution to the Indian problem and chiding General Crook when it appeared that officer was not pursuing the Apaches with the relentless determination which alone, Marion believed, would bring an end to the settlers' troubles. He continued to rejoice over mineral discoveries, to publish glowing accounts of the rich crops raised in the Prescott area, to chastise the Republicans for the errors of their ways and altogether to provide a lively picture of the development of Prescott and central Arizona.

In 1873 Marion married Flora E. Banghart, daughter of his good friend George Banghart.[9] They had three children, George Crook, named for the general, Louis E. and Edmund who died in infancy. In addition to his newspaper Marion operated a ranch on lower Granite Creek near its junction with the Verde. The *Miner* of February 4, 1876 reported he had a herd of 2,200 sheep and a cozy home. The columns of the paper are also full of the comings and goings of the Marions between Prescott and the ranch, of visits to Chino Valley and domestic details of a busy, growing family. Marion was at various times county treasurer and legislator, and it was

---

[9]See note 7 to the text following.

through his efforts as a member of the Ninth Legislature that the capital was moved back to Prescott briefly before being moved permanently to Phoenix in 1889.

Tragedy — certainly it was so considered eighty years ago — struck the life of this solid citizen and community leader in November, 1884 when Flora Banghart Marion disappeared from Prescott in the company of District Attorney Charles B. Rush whom Marion had just supported in his campaign for office. Arizona papers expressed sympathy for the families involved, regret at the conduct of the guilty couple and dropped the matter. Marion instituted proceedings for divorce which was granted in 1887, and in April 1888 he married Ida Jones, "a former typo in the Courier office." A son, John H. Jr. was born in May of 1889.

On the morning of July 27, 1891 Marion went to the well at the rear of his home to draw a pail of water. As he was returning to the house he collapsed and died on the porch steps before anyone could reach him. His funeral was one of the largest Prescott had ever seen, and all business was suspended during the services.

"The news of the death of old John Marion," wrote John G. Bourke, "comes to one like a crushing blow. I knew and loved him for twenty-two years. When the history of Arizona shall be written, no name will shine with more luster on its pages than that of our friend. He was one of God's noblemen."[10]

*   *   *   *

The text of Marion's travel account has been transcribed from a photostat of the copy in the Denver Public Library. It differs in some but not significant details from the account as printed in the columns of the *Miner.* A very few obviously typographical errors have been corrected.

Donald M. Powell
Tucson, 1965

---

[10]*Courier,* August 24, 1891.

TRAVELS THROUGH ARIZONA.

INTRODUCTION.

When the following narrative first appeared, in weekly instalments, in the MINER, the writer had little hope that it would please anybody, or that it could be of service to Arizona, but having recently received orders for numbers of the MINER containing it, and being unable to furnish them, we have, at the request of personal friends and well-wishers of Arizona, printed a sufficient number of copies to meet all demands, and having done so, we hope to be pardoned for expressing the wish that our crude pamphlet will meet with ready sale, and be of some service to Arizona and her people.

THE PARTY.

Consisted of Colonel George Stoneman, Military Commander of the Department of Arizona; Major M. Cogswell, 21st Infantry, Inspector; Surgeon H. R. Wirtz, U. S. A., Medical Director; Geo. H. Kimball, of Camp Date Creek, three servants, one cook, twelve enlisted men of M Troop, 3d Cavalry, four teamsters, and our humble self, making in all, twenty-five men. We had two ambulances, each of which was drawn by four stout, active mules. Each wagon was drawn by six mules.

THE START.

Was made from Fort Whipple about eleven o'clock in the forenoon of Monday, August 29, 1870, and though the friends we left behind had some serious misgivings about our making the trip, and escaping the shafts and bullets of hostile Indians, no such misgivings rested in our breasts. Indeed, we thought ourselves numerous enough, and brave enough, too, to take care of ourselves and animals, and yet, all realized the fact that it was a dangerous undertaking. But, thank God, we got through safely, with but few accidents, and no visible peril to life.

The day was a fine one in every respect—a true type of those beautiful summer days of ours, and as we turned to look at picturesque Whipple, neat and cozy Prescott, and the dark, rounded, Sierra Prieta range of mountains, we could not but realize the fact that we were fast traveling from home and friends into a strange, mysterious country, peopled with savages, the most treacherous on the continent. Nevertheless, we did not regret the fact. Indeed it rather pleased us to know that we were on the road, bounding along over grassy plains—free as the breeze which swept over them. We had not gone far on our journey when accidents No. 1 occurred, and we were stopped in our course. A sand-board of a wagon broke; the wagon was unloaded, an axe and a piece of wood were procured, and the work of repairing damages was commenced by Col. Stoneman, who, with his own hands, fixed the thing in short order, and we were about ready to start when it was discovered that a mule which one of the men rode was lacking in strength and spirit, and could not possibly make the trip. Rider and mule were sent back to Whipple. The rider carried a note to Capt. Foster, requesting that gentleman to give him another and better mule; also, to send us some hard timber for sand-boards, etc. It was about dark when we encamped below the ranches in Chino Valley, but not too late for us to start on a foraging expedition. We first went to the house of Jas. Baker, where we procured two canteens of milk, which we carried to the mess and delivered to that greatest of caterers, Dr. Wirtz. Having received an invitation from George Banghart to pass the night under his hospitable roof, we bade good night to our fellow-voyagers, and started for Mr. Banghart's, where we were kindly treated and entertained by that gentleman and his estimable wife. During the night, Capt. Foster and one or two mechanics came up, with material and tools, and fixed our demoralized wagon. As we did not get a very early start, our party had a good chance to look around the valley—to admire the fine corn, etc., the beautiful young cottonwood trees that grow around the fields, and those immense springs of pure, cold water, from which issue sufficient water to irrigate thousands of acres and supply a large city. The verdict of the officers was that Chino Valley was the prettiest agricultural settlement they had seen in the Territory. Distance traveled, first day, about twenty miles.

INTRODUCTION

When the following narrative first appeared, in weekly instalments, in the *Miner,* the writer had little hope that it would
please anybody, or that it could be of service to Arizona, but
having recently received orders for numbers of the *Miner*
containing it, and being unable to furnish them, we have, at
the request of personal friends and well-wishers of Arizona,
printed a sufficient number of copies to meet all demands,
and having done so, we hope to be pardoned for expressing
the wish that our crude pamphlet will meet with ready sale,
and be of some service to Arizona and her people:

THE PARTY

consisted of Colonel George Stoneman, Military Commander
of the Department of Arizona;[1] Major M. Cogswell, 21st
Infantry, Inspector;[2] Surgeon H. R. Wirtz, U.S.A., Medical
Director;[3] Geo. H. Kimball, of Camp Date Creek,[4] three servants, one cook, twelve enlisted men of M Troop, 3d Cavalry,
four teamsters, and our humble self, making in all twenty-five
men. We had two ambulances, each of which was drawn by
four stout, active mules. Each wagon was drawn by six mules.

THE START

was made from Fort Whipple about eleven o'clock in the
forenoon of Monday, August 29, 1870, and though the friends
we left behind had some serious misgivings about our making
the trip, and escaping the shafts and bullets of hostile Indians,
no such misgivings rested in our breasts. Indeed, we thought
ourselves numerous enough, and brave enough, too, to take
care of ourselves and animals, and yet, all realized the fact
that it was a dangerous undertaking. But, thank God, we got

through safely, with but few accidents, and no visible peril to life.

The day was a fine one in every respect — a true type of those beautiful summer days of ours, and as we turned to look at picturesque Whipple, neat and cozy Prescott, and the dark, rounded, Sierra Prieta range of mountains, we could not but realize the fact that we were fast traveling from home and friends into a strange, mysterious country, peopled with savages, the most treacherous on the continent. Nevertheless, we did not regret the fact. Indeed it rather pleased us to know that we were on the road, bounding along over grassy plains — free as the breeze which swept over them. We had not gone far on our journey when accident No. 1 occurred, and we were stopped in our course. A sand-board of a wagon broke; the wagon was unloaded, an axe and a piece of wood were procured, and the work of repairing damages was commenced by Col. Stoneman, who, with his own hands, fixed the thing in short order,[5] and we were about ready to start when it was discovered that a mule which one of the men rode was lacking in strength and spirit and could not possibly make the trip. Rider and mule were sent back to Whipple. The rider carried a note to Capt. Foster, requesting that gentleman to give him another and better mule; also, to send us some hard timber for sand-boards, etc. It was about dark when we encamped below the ranches in Chino Valley, but not too late for us to start on a foraging expedition. We first went to the house of Jas. Baker,[6] where we procured two canteens of milk, which we carried to the mess and delivered to that greatest of caterers, Dr. Wirtz. Having received an invitation from George Banghart[7] to pass the night under his hospitable roof, we bade good night to our fellow-voyagers, and started for Mr. Banghart's, where we were kindly treated and entertained by that gentleman and his estimable wife. During the night, Capt. Foster and one or two mechanics came up, with material and tools, and fixed our demoralized wagon. As we did not get a very early start, our party had a good chance to look around the valley — to admire the fine corn, etc., the beautiful young cottonwood trees that grew around the fields, and those immense springs of pure, cold water, from which issue sufficient water to irrigate thousands of acres and supply a large city. The verdict of the officers was that Chino Valley was the prettiest agricultural settlement they had seen in the Territory. Distance traveled, first day, about *twenty miles.*

Tuesday, August 30. After bidding adieu to friends, we started from the last settlement we were destined to see for hundreds of miles, and wended our way northward towards the San Francisco and Bill Williams Mountains. For the first few miles the road remained good and smooth, but after that we struck into a trap country, and terrific were the joltings we received, as the wagons pitched and heaved over large, hard-headed and hard-hearted bowlders — known to some folk as "nigger-heads."[8] We soon reached that venerable, terrible old box in the earth, known as "Hell Cañon,"[9] and in going down its southern side, met with accident No. 2, *i.e.* the upsetting of a wagon, which, luckily, caused no serious trouble, and broke nothing. After passing this fearful chasm, we drove about one mile and encamped in a beautiful grassy spot, surrounded by juniper trees, near some water tanks, around which were bones of horses, mules and oxen, which Lo, the poor Indian had stolen and eaten. The country passed over to-day is admirably adapted to stock raising, grass being abundant, and water plenty in tanks in the cañons. We had a splendid view of the country to the East and West, saw the great and productive Chino Valley, stretching away to the West; likewise the fine large valley that stretches away to the Verde river, and which, with its thick, rich coating of green grass, its groves of juniper and cedars, pleased the eye, and filled the mind with visions of flocks and herds, which, ere long, are destined to feed upon it. The surface of the ground in this vicinity is covered with trap bowlders and debris, and it is a very unpleasant region to ride over in wagons. Distance traveled, about *twelve miles.*

Wednesday, August 31. Our road, to-day, wound through

"the Cedars," which are of good size, and cover the entire face of the country. As trap continued to be "the formation," the reader may well believe we had a rough road, over which it was impossible to make good time. To-day, another sand-board gave way, and, as usual, was repaired by Col. Stone-man. While traveling along, a band of deer was seen scamper-ing over the hills. Grass was plenty on some portions of the day's drive, and scarce on others. We arrived at Bear Springs,[10] in the pine timber, about five o'clock, after a tiresome jour-ney. The water from these springs runs south towards the Verde, and is plenty and good. Distance traveled, fully *eighteen miles.*

Thursday, Sept. 1. The camp was aroused long before daylight, everything got in readiness, and we started just as the sun peered over the great mountain range to the east of us. The road to-day was through mountains, which were cov-ered with nutritious grasses, and a very heavy growth of large pine trees. Clover was plenty in the small valleys; water was found in tanks, and the day's journey would have been a delightful one but for the rocky nature of the greater portion of the country passed over. We reached Leroux Springs[11] and valley early in the afternoon, when the Colonel, with his usual precaution and foresight, selected a good and safe camp. The water at this point was good and plenty, as were also, the grass and pine timber, and we are very sure that, for boldness, grandeur and impressiveness, the scenery is equal to that of any other portion of the continent. In front and west-ward of our camp lay an immense valley, hemmed in by pine-clad hills, and sentineled, as it were, by lofty peaks, the high-est and most prominent of which were the three bald, wedge-shaped ones known as the San Francisco Mountains. Bill Wil-liams Mountain, southwest from camp, was barely visible, and presented a very rugged appearance. Distance made, about *twenty miles.*

Friday, September 2. Got an early start, as usual. Trav-eled across Leroux valley, in which we found plenty of excel-lent water, and an immense hole in the ground — an extinct crater — which, no doubt, in times past, vomited forth huge streams of molten lava. After leaving the valley, our route led around the western base of the San Francisco Mountain, through the largest, straightest kind of pine timber. It was late in the afternoon when we arrived at Antelope Springs,[12] on the northeast side of San Francisco Mountain, and encamped, near an old abandoned stage station, not far from the great mountain, which is said to be 12,000 feet in hight [sic]. Our camp being a mile or more from the springs, we had some difficulty in finding water, but got enough for all purposes in a ravine near camp. For a high mountain country — the highest in Arizona — water was scarce, and the grass quite dry, proving conclusively that but little rain had fallen on the northern side of the mountain the past summer. The nights were exceedingly cool, days very pleasant. Road, to-day, pretty good. Formation, trap. Distance traveled, *twenty-four miles.*

   Saturday, September 3. This day's march brought to view some peculiar sights. We had become tired of gazing at huge mountains and pine trees, and felt relieved when, after traveling some eight or ten miles, cedar and juniper took the place of the pine, and the country to the north and east opened to onr view, displaying jagged peaks and points, round, detached mountains, in which holes or depressions were observed, and which were formerly active volcanos. One of these — the most perfect type of extinct volcano on the continent, was sketched by Dr. Wirtz, and the sketch, with others, will shortly be transferred to the pages of some leading magazine.[13]

   It may be guessed, from the foregoing, that the country passed over on this day's march was covered with lava, yet grass of good quality was plenty, and an abundance of pure water was found in tanks at Cosnino Caves.[14] These caves are large and numerous, and were, no doubt, once inhabited by the Cosnino Indians, who still visit them. The tanks, containing the water, are immense holes in the bed-rock of a large, dry stream, and are somewhat difficult of approach, being guarded by the high, rocky sides and falls of the creek.

Various patches of this section of Arizona are covered with black, volcanic sand.

After watering our animals and filling our vessels with that best — most necessary of all liquids — water, we drove on over a poor country, and arrived early in the afternoon at the old stage station on Cañon Diablo,[15] where we found a little water in round holes in the solid trap rock that formed the bed of the cañon. These holes, which had been formed by the action of water turning pebbles and bowlders — making them spin around — were from one to four feet deep, and about one foot in diameter at their tops, while the bottoms were quite small. We found here good grass, and gave the animals the benefit of it. Distance made, about *twenty-eight miles.*

Sunday, September 4. This was our first Sunday in the wilderness, that is, on the present journey, and the day was spent in traveling over a bad road and poor country. The fact is, this section of Arizona is not of much account, and we longed to get over it. So we traveled as fast as the nature of the country would admit, and late in the afternoon, encamped on the banks of the Little Colorado, or as some call it, Flax River, which gets its principal supply of water from the northern side of the Mogollon and Sierra Blanco ranges of mountains. Before reaching the river, we passed through a low range of sand hills, the material of which had been hardened by exposure, etc., and curious were the shapes into which the sides of the hills had been *carved* by the action of the rain. Series and groups of large and small cellules met the eye in every direction, and with the curious shapes of the deep red rocks presented a picture the like of which is not often seen. Here, indeed, nature has labored with curious, unique effect. While going through these rocks — tracks of Indians were discovered. Previous to reaching them, we passed over a country covered with flat, volcanic stone, in passing over which the sound made by the vehicles led one to imagine that there were caverns underneath. Near the river we came across a slough, containing some water, and a great deal of mud. We passed over it in safety, after some difficulty and were, for the first time, in the valley of the Little Colorado, within sight of the timber on its banks, and eager to get a look at the stream itself, but our curiosity was not satisfied until we had gone several miles, for the water runs through a cañon which had to be headed before the river became accessible. After a march of about *thirty miles,* the road turned straight to the river, and stopped on its banks, when all got a sight at and a drink of the water, which proved to be better than we had expected. In fact, it contained nothing deleterious except a little alkali, which only had the effect of making us drink the more. The stream is not by any means a large one on the surface, but its bed being of quick sand, it was easy for us to perceive that here, at least, fully as much water as was running upon the surface, was invisible below, in the mud and sand.

Monday, September 5. Traveled up west side of Little Colorado, a great part of the way over barren, alkaline flats. About noon, accident No. 4 occurred, which was the heating of a spindle belonging to the Colonel's ambulance. Luckily, we were not far from the river when the wheel refused to turn, and Colonel Stoneman was not long in rigging a purchase which enabled us to get the ambulance to Sunset Crossing,[16] where a huge fire was kindled, the spindle heated and made as good as new. While this work was going on the ford was tried, and found passable. A note from Lieutenant Upham, 3d Cavalry,[17], who had come down from Camp Mogollon[18] to meet the party, was found. It stated that the Lieutenant and his men were about out of rations and could not wait for the party. This was discouraging, and the Colonel sent a Sergeant and one man to overhaul the Lieutenant. After crossing the river, our party traveled through some fine valleys — over which the river, when on a bender, had swept. Grass was plenty. We passed, on road, a small, dirty stream of water, running from the east which must be Navajo Creek.[19] We made, to-day, about *thirty miles.*

Tuesday, September 6. Followed up river to Leroux crossing,[20] where we came up with the men who had been sent to overhaul Lieutenant Upham and party, but who did not do so, the Lieutenant having broke camp before their arrival. This was discouraging news. We had now to leave the river, and traverse a mountainous country without road or guide, and all through a mistake, if not a blunder, on the part of those who were ordered to wait at this point for the Colonel. But we will do as did the Colonel, pass it over, and as we are about to enter a new and very different region of the country from that which we have traversed, we will go back on the route and "bring up" some matters of importance to the reader. As the new road now being built from Camp Verde will cross the river near this point, it may not be out of place to compare the two routes and the regions through which they pass. We had now traveled about 212 miles, mostly through a mountainous country, which we did not find very well supplied with water, but in which, at most seasons, there is *too much water.* Of course, wells might be sunk, and water found at almost any point, but that would not make a good all the year route of it, for the snows of winter would be a bar thereto, and it would cost thousands of dollars to make a good wagon-road over the great extent of country, from which the trap bowlders would have to be removed. On the contrary, the new route, is in a measure free from trap, is better watered, well grassed and crosses the Mogollon chain of mountains far below the altitude at which the old route crosses the San Francisco Mountains. Besides, it is nearly *one hundred miles* shorter, the distance from Prescott to the crossing of the Little Colorado, by this route, being about 120 miles, against 212, the length of the old route. As work upon this new route is now being pushed to completion, we can soon congratulate ourselves upon having a practicable wagon-road connecting us with Santa Fe, New Mexico, distance 420 miles, or 100 miles less than the old, rocky, sky-scraping San Francisco route. This new route was found and located by Capt. Hawley, 3d Cavalry, as was also the route to Camp Mogollon [now Camp Thomas] which leaves the river at this point. Distance made, about *thirty miles.*

Wednesday, September 7. Crossed to west side of the river, about noon; followed level, grassy plain for about *sixteen miles,* when we encamped late at night, without water. Formation sand-stone and trap.

Thursday, September 8. Started about daylight, and traveled through sand-stone country, covered with good grass and juniper trees. Encamped late in the afternoon in a large, beautiful valley at the head of the Cañon of Chevelon's Fork of the Little Colorado, after a march of about *twenty miles,* six or eight of which we might have saved, had we not followed tracks made by Lieut. Upham's party.[21]

Chevelon's Fork — the stream upon which we camped, is a large, bold, dashing mountain stream, running about 1,000 inches of water, in which sport numberless fish, resembling mountain trout. Upon it are large, fine valleys, and the grazing for miles on either side is excellent. Our camp was about eighteen miles from the Little Colorado, and from it to that river, the water of Chevelon's Fork passes through a rough-looking cañon in sand-stone hills. The weather, during the night, was cool, ice having formed upon some water, in a large tin pan. Timber was abundant in the hills.

Friday, September 9. Crossed to east side of Chevelon's Fork, and wended our way over rough bowlders, through pine and cedar, sometimes close to the stream; sometimes one and two miles away from it. Passed on the road many fine springs, and after traveling about *eighteen miles,* encamped in a delightful country, at a point where the waters of the river boil up, after having ran [sic] for some distance under the trap, from the mountains above. These springs are the largest ever seen by us. The water is delicious; the country adjacent magnificent, therefore, it cannot long remain unsettled.

Saturday, September 10. This day's journey south, was a hard one for the animals. We made *twenty-seven miles,* over a rough, rocky country, mostly through tall pine timber, and shortly after crossing the divide of the great Mogollon range of mountains, encamped on the headwaters of the North

Fork of White Mountain river,[22] in a delightful mountain region. While crossing the summit of the Mogollon, we had a fine view of the country, and a glorious country it was. Northwest and southeast, far as the eye was able to reach, there appeared one interminable forest of pine, oak and cedar, with here and there tall peaks. Southward, for miles, the same view was presented; northward, the view was not as pleasing. But little timber was visible, and the only objects that attracted the attention or pleased the eye, were jagged, fanciful peaks and hills away in the country of the Moquis. We climbed a hill near camp, and got a fine view of the White Mountain peaks, the second highest in Arizona. Formation sand-stone and trap, mostly the latter.

Sunday, September 11. Traveled south, through a fine forest, in which were springs, small lakes, and beautiful meadows. Formation, red sand-stone and trap. Reached Camp Mogollon,[23] after a ride of *seventeen miles,* and were highly pleased at seeing white men and women once again. On our way down, we passed a log corral, which the writer of this helped build, in the fall of '66,[24] while "hunting for gold," which was not found. Distance from the Little Colorado, by the tortuous route we had traveled, about 98 miles, which, when added to the 212 miles from Prescott to the last crossing of the river, makes the entire distance traveled in fourteen days, 310 miles, or a little over 22 miles a day. This too, with heavily laden wagons and ambulances, over the roughest country on the continent, and with animals which, since leaving Chino Valley, had not seen a kernel of grain. Yet, thanks to the good grass on the entire route, our mules arrived at Mogollon in almost as good condition as when they were given to us at Fort Whipple by that honest, capable Quartermaster, Capt. C. W. Foster.[25]

CAMP MOGOLLON, (NOW CAMP THOMAS)

is pleasantly situated on the southern side of a large stream, known as the east fork of White Mountain River. This fork rises in the White or Sierra Blanca Mountains, which are in plain view of the post, to the north. The north fork rises in the Mogollon range, but gets considerable water from the Sierra Blanca. Both streams unite a short distance below the post, and form the White Mountain river, which flows westwardly into the Prieta, or Salt River. All these streams are well stocked with trout. The country on every side of the post is heavily timbered, and grass is plenty. Bear, elk, deer, antelope, turkey, Indians, and other wild game are numerous. The climate is similar to that of Prescott, and altogether, it is a paradise of a place, as is the entire country on every side of it. Officers and men were living in tents, and the only houses that had been erected were those used by the Quartermaster and Post Trader. The latter gentleman had a fine house nearly completed, for a store and lager-beer brewery, and was brewing the first lager ever brewed in that region, when we arrived. The post was garrisoned by three small companies, L. and M. 1st Cavalry, and B, of the 21st Infantry. Major John Green,[26] 1st Cav., was in command, and from what we saw and learned we have no hesitancy in pronouncing him an able, dignified officer. His services against the Indians are well known to our people. The other officers of the post were Captains J. C. Hunt, John Barry, and H. E. Smith; Lieutenants, M. Harris, Acting Quartermaster and Commissary, F. K. Upham, and Dr. J. C. Handy, all first-rate, stirring officers.[27]

THE INDIANS

had not changed much since last we saw them, in 1866, but we missed some familiar faces, and as the members of the tribe present could give no straight account of their whereabouts, the conclusion forced itself upon us that they had fallen while raiding upon the whites. The supposition was current that all the Indians around the post were Coyotero Apaches, which might be correct. We circulated about the post considerably during the evening of our first day there, and gleaned some facts regarding our red brethren and the country, the relation of which may prove interesting to our readers: First, then, our informants, who appeared to be pretty well posted, assured us that the Coyotero band or tribe numbered nearly six thousand souls, 1,500 of whom might be classed as warriors, but we think this an over-estimate. They have four principal chiefs; Eskelthesala, whose chieftaincy came down to him from his ancestors, Pedro, Miguel, and Chiquita Captain.[28] Miguel has but one eye, but manages to see clearer with that than do any of his brother chiefs with their two eyes. In a word, he is by far the shrewdest, ablest Indian of the tribe. The Coyoteros profess to be at peace with the whites, but those who know them best, look upon this profession as a good joke. Eskelthesala and his followers have for years been friendly to us, not for any love they have for us, but from motives of policy, and no truer idea of the sentiments of the majority of the tribe can be given than the fact that Eskelthesala, whom they once reverenced, and styled "Captain Grande," has sank into insignificance and disrepute among them. Yet, we have some faith in the peaceful professions of most of the leading chiefs, and believe we can ally them to us by treating them squarely and properly; that is by keeping a respectable number of troops in their country, assisting them to raise crops and live, furnish them with medicines, and seeing that they stay at home, and do not steal away on expeditions. When all this is done, the Coyoteros may act honestly. Their country is a delightful one, and to their credit be it said, they are passionately fond of it. Go where you will through it, you will find plenty of game, grass, timber and water, with sufficient agricultural land to produce food for thousands of people. They know how to raise corn, wheat and vegetables, at least the women do, and although, of late years, they have had bad luck with their crops, they yet have corn and fodder to sell to the post. We know it to be the fixed opinion of most Arizonians that the Apache cannot be tamed, but proper measures for doing so have never before been taken, and it may be that this opinion will soon be abandoned. We hope so, at all events, for it is cheaper, better for the country to feed and civilize them than it is to fight them, which latter mode of dealing with them has so far proved an expensive, ineffectual way of subduing them. The Coyoteros, speak the same language as their friends and our enemies, the Pinalenos and Tontos, and, perhaps the Apache Mohave, which latter tribe is now nominally at peace with us. All being Apaches, they visit each other, intermarry, and get along swimmingly together, so that it looks ridiculous to be at peace with one clan, allow them to become acquainted with our ways and means, while fighting their friends and brothers. Yet, the Coyoteros assert that the other clans are anxious to make peace with us, but the recent murders and robberies committed by them do not look much like it. All Apaches are on good terms with the Zuni and Moquis Indians, and a brisk trade is kept up between them. On the contrary, the powerful Navajo tribe — once part and parcel of the Apache nation, and now speaking the same language, are deadly foes to the Apaches, kill them whenever and wherever they can, and rob them at every opportunity. The Navajoes are also the scourge of the Moquis and Zunis, and being brave Indians, all others are afraid of them. But a little while ago a party of these king robbers killed a Coyotero and stole a horse, and soon after, cut down the wheat which the poor Zunis had growing, and packed it away with them. The Coyoteros — male and female — are a hardy, good-looking, intelligent race of Indians. The women are noted for their virtue and industry. The men spend their time in gambling and lazing around, when not out hunting and stealing. They manufacture, from untanned buckskin, very good monte "cards," a pack of which was secured by Dr. Wirtz. They are exceedingly suspicious, superstitious and religious, consequently, have great faith in and reverence for their medicine men, and "prophets." If memory serves us right, they deposit their dead in caverns in rocks, together with their personal effects. We tried to find out something concerning our near and very dear neighbors, *"The Pinalenos and Tontos,"* but

only heard that the Pinalenos could, perhaps, muster 1,500
warriors, which, if true, is bad for us, for they are a villian-
ous [sic] set of robbers and murderers.

Monday, September 12, was spent in camp, repairing
wagons and shoeing animals. Major Cogswell, who by the
way, had all the work of inspecting to do, was kept busy per-
forming that duty. The troops were reviewed early in the
morning, and went through the evolutions like veterans, as
they were. Col. Stoneman and Dr. Wirtz were not idle, and
we are sure that Mr. Kimball busied himself in looking
around, watching for chances to enrich himself by furnishing
our good Uncle with something he needed. We, actually, had
nothing to do, and did it admirably.

Tuesday, September 13, opened brightly upon camp,
and we awoke with the first tap of the drum, ate a hearty
breakfast and started down the river to look up a new site for
a post; that is, Col. Stoneman, Major Cogswell, Major Green,
Captain Smith, and all the doctors, went for that purpose,
and we accompanied them, so as to be on hand to record any
accident that might occur, for there was a steep cañon in
front of the new site, whose depth had to be determined, in
doing which it was not improbable that some of the officers
might fall down and break their necks. The new site gave
entire satisfaction to all, and Col. Stoneman accepted it for
the future home of his braves. It is a large, high mesa, 100
feet above the level of the stream, and cannot be other than
a healthy location.[29]

AN INDIAN POW-WOW

was to take place this forenoon, and when our party got back
to camp, many big and little Indians were squatted under the
trees, near Col. Stoneman's tent, anxious to shake hands with
him, and eager to "talk" in their smooth, mild dialect. After
the usual presentations were made, Mr. Miguel "took the
floor," and addressing himself to Chairman Stoneman, said,
in substance, that he was glad to see him; God had made men

differently; the white man He made rich; the red poor, which was all a mistake on Miguel's part. But, he continued, "Last year I made peace with Col. Green, and have been a good man ever since."

Monsieur Eskelthesala spoke next. He commenced by saying he had much to say, and was going to say it, which remark made us feel uneasy, for we were anxious to get on the road, and strike homewards. But he continued, and we were forced to listen to the old barbarian. The veins in his aged neck swelled until they were as large as a man's fingers, his mouth opened and he said he had "heard a good deal about Stoneman, and was glad to see him. God had brought them together to smoke in peace (a gentle hint for some cigarritoes, which were immediately furnished and passed around), and what he (Eskelthesala,) had said or might say, would be written on stone and he thought it would last." Of course this saying was merely a figure of speech, for neither the old fellow nor any of his tribe understand the art of writing on stone or anything else. Then, in token of his love for the rations of beef that had been given him, he said he "was always glad to get to eat meat, that snow would soon come, and his people would need clothing; once they were rich in horses, mules, asses and cattle, and could trade with the Zunis for everything they needed — powder and lead included — now they were poor, the soldiers and the frost having destroyed their crops, and they wanted assistance, aye, even powder and lead "to kill game with."

Pedro, who appeared to advantage in a clean suit of mantua, commenced in a begging strain. His people wanted more rations, guns, powder, lead and clothing. He declaimed against the Navajos, and wanted them kept on their reservation, or, if that could not be done, leave to fight them and steal from them. He wanted a physician and an Indian agent for his people, and expressed a laudable desire to learn something about two Indians whom he once sent to Tucson with an express, and who, it is said, were massacreed [*sic*] near that place. He furthermore said that Ca-Cheis — the Indians call him "Cheis," had visited Col. Green, and was anxious to make peace with the Americans, and that he believed Cheis meant what he had said. He then spoke about the Pinals, and said that all but one chief were tired of war. Pedro then subsided, and Miguel opened in a new vein. He wanted hoes, axes, and other tools for his people, so that they could till the ground and make themselves comfortable.

This speech pleased Col. Stoneman better than all the rest. He inquired if they (the Chiefs) had said all they desired. They had. Col. Stoneman then commenced by promising to do all he could for Indians who would live in peace with the whites. "God," he said, "wants all people to live together in peace. Away to the East, were myriads of white men, and in one big city, lived the Great Father of all Indians and Americans, (meaning Ulysses) who would do right by both." This appeared to please the reds, who grunted their approval. He then said that should the Navajos continue to war upon them he would issue orders to commanders of posts to send their soldiers against the Navajos; advised them to abandon the foolish custom of burning the clothing of Indians who might die, as it would keep them poor and naked; said he would keep on giving them rations of meat and, perhaps, flour, provided they would remain peaceable and assist the troops in hunting and killing bad Indians; tried to impress them with the idea of the great cost to the government of flour, beef, etc.; promised them seed corn, etc., and hoped that hereafter, they would raise enough grain and vegetables to feed themselves; said the business of the soldiers was to kill bad Indians, and protect citizens, and that if they did not behave themselves, stop stealing from posts and settlements, they would all get killed; in two months, he would be prepared to furnish them medicines, and would also write to Washington, for an Indian agent for them.

The Colonel's talk being ended, Miguel with fitting words and great tact asked the Colonel what he designed doing with Barbashay, an old and bad Pinal Chief who was then in the guard-house, in a wilted condition. After inquiring about the case, the Colonel asked Miguel what he would like to see done with him. Miguel would not say, further than that the prisoner was in the Colonel's power; that he had been a bad Indian, but, was then, and would be thereafter, incapable of doing harm, for the very good reason that he was in feeble health, and could not possibly live long. Finally, Miguel acknowledged that he wished Barbashay set at liberty, and would go security for his good behaviour in future, if the Colonel demanded it. But, he first wished to give Barbashay "a piece of his mind." In answer to this proposition, Col. Stoneman said, in substance, "I will release him, and if he should choose to keep on fighting, let him do so, and get killed." This pleased the Indians, and they applauded with a vim. After a general handshaking, the conference broke up, we repaired to our ambulances, bade good-bye to friends and started for Camp Goodwin, never stopping until we arrived late in the afternoon, on the banks of that noble stream, the Prieta, or Salt River. Distance traveled, *eighteen miles,* over a very rough country, containing plenty of wood, water and grass. During the night, Paymaster Morrow and Hon. Sylvester Mowry[30] arrived, and told us the news.

Wednesday, September 14. Crossed Salt River and Natanes range[31] of mountains. Road, to-day, wound through pine and cedar, over rough trap rock, and steep hills, which made it quite bad. Country delightful. Camped at night on top of hills overlooking the Gila, where, for the first time since leaving Prescott, water and grass were scarce. Made about *twenty-five miles.*

Thursday, September 15. Made about 20 *miles,* and arrived at Camp Goodwin[32] about one o'clock in the afternoon, where we found two small companies of troops, commanded by Lieutenants Pollock and Robinson. As usual, nearly every man, woman and child in the garrison were sick with fever, and Col. Stoneman gave orders for the abandonment of the terrible "Black Hole," as soon as the public property could be removed to Camp Thomas. When this became known, officers and soldiers *shook* for joy, and the post surgeon, Dr. Baker, felt mighty good. This sickly post has caused the death of many brave men, and it was an act of mercy on the part of the Colonel to abandon it. It is near the Gila river, on a small stream called the Tularosa; is an extensive adobe establishment, and with the beautiful shade trees surrounding it, would be a little paradise, but for the climate, which is hotter than Tophet, and the sickness which attacks all who stay there over night. Near it, on the south and east, are two huge mountains — Graham and Trumbull. Major Cogswell caught the fever, and having to inspect troops, etc., in the hot sun, suffered considerably. Our party met with very kind treatment from the officers and post trader, Mr. Lacy.[39] Mr. Kimball, who had accompanied us from Prescott to this point, and who proved to be a very agreeable companion, left us here, with the intention of going direct to Tucson with Major Morrow.

It commenced raining during the afternoon of the day we reached Goodwin, and continued to do so nearly the whole of the night, which pleased the garrison, the more so as but little rain had descended during the summer months. Before and during the rain-storm, sky and earth were frequently emblazoned with lightning, and peals of thunder reverberated from mountain to mountain. During the afternoon, a black pall overhung the Sierra Blanca country, to the northwest, and the rain must have descended there in torrents. A rainbow — with all its colors — floated in mid air over the Gila mountains, and added new beauties to the gorgeous sky that developed at sunset, when there was a lull in the rain storm and a light breeze drove the black clouds back over the high sierras. Glad were we for being on the south side of the Gila, and for having no large streams ahead of us to cross, for we had before experienced great difficulty in crossing the White Mountain streams, and traveling through the country, during wet weather.

Friday, September 16. The morning of this day opened cool and clear, and although the previous night had been a pleasant one, for Camp Goodwin, we did not rest well in the adobe buildings; the atmosphere of which was anything but comfortable and refreshing. But good coffee, broiled chicken, and other nice things — furnished by Lieutenant Robinson, induced considerable vigor, and we turned our backs on the feverish spot with unspeakable delight, followed up through the large, rich valleys of the Gila, over a muddy road, for about *thirty miles,* when we encamped within sight of the river, not far from the ancient city known as "Pueblo Biejo."[34] In following the Gila, this day, we passed over some excellent farming and grazing lands. Cottonwood and mesquite were plenty, and the nutritious beans that had grown upon the latter trees lay thickly strewn upon the ground. As there are those who have never seen mesquite, we will endeavor to describe it. First, then, it is an evergreen, with crooked trunk, which frequently runs up ten and twelve feet without a limb; the branches are quite numerous; the leaves tiny. All over it are numerous thorns, sharp as pins, and stout enough to make themselves felt. It makes the very best firewood and when we take into consideration the valuable beans it bears and the cool shade it affords the weary traveler, the mesquite with all its thorns — is a beautiful, valuable tree. It flourishes best in the vicinity of Tucson, where there are immense forests along the Santa Cruz,[35] but it grows all over Southern Arizona. Cottonwoods, of large size, cover the banks and bottoms of the Gila, and with the green grass, water, etc., form a pleasing contrast to the black hills on either side, that is, at this point, for [*sic*] above it, for over two hundred miles, valleys and hills are clothed with green grass the year round, and timber is more frequently met with on the hills. A short distance below Goodwin, the river wends its way through a great cañon, several miles in length. There is one more cañon above, between Pueblo Biejo and old Fort West,[36] a distance of nearly two hundred miles. In 1866, when we traveled down the Gila, from West to Goodwin, we took particular notice of the country, and think now, as we did then, that the Upper Gila country will yet swarm with industrious whites. Into it empty several large streams — the largest of which is the Bonita, upon which stream, it is said, Cheis and his tribe wish to settle and live in peace. The mountains south of the Gila, in this vicinity, are formed of granite, and there is a great deal of float quartz.

Saturday, September 17. Five o'clock in the morning found us ready to travel; we turned our backs upon the "Sacred Gila," and entering San Simeon Valley, [*sic*] just as the sun was getting out of his blankets, which must have been worn threadbare, or made damp by the recent rains, for the old fire god presented a rather chilly appearance. After traveling about *fifteen miles,* we reached some water holes, where men and animals rested and refreshed themselves. By this time the sun had grown warm, and as there was not so much as a mesquite tree in sight of camp, in the valley, our little party had to pile close together under the wagons and ambulances. But it did not take the animals long to fill themselves with the rich grasses which grew all over the valley, and after filling the canteens, etc., we hitched up, started, went about fifteen miles and made a "dry" camp. Distance traveled, about *thirty miles.*

Sunday, September 18, opened bright and beautiful, and we were not long in getting on the road. As some of our party had been to Camp Bowie, prominent landmarks near that post were pointed out, and we knew that the place was not far off. Col. Stoneman, who was one of the first Americans to travel through this region, recognized the famous Stein's Peak, Cathedral Rock, *Dos Cabezes* [*sic*] etc. We passed Graham Mountain, which had stuck to us, or, rather we to it, since leaving Camp Goodwin, and saw between it and the Chiricahua Mountains, a long, narrow valley, through which the route of the 32d parallel railroad passes, and known as Railroad Pass. We soon entered Ewell's, now Apache Pass,[37] and memory reverting to the horrid deeds that had therein been enacted, by Apaches, a feeling of insecurity came over us, and our eyes kept busy watch for the red-skins. The road from San Simeon valley, winds around through a narrow pass or cañon, along the bed of a creek, for some five or six miles, when it ascends rolling hills. Bowie is located upon one of those hills, a little south of the road, and a short distance east of the springs which form the creek.[38] In going up to the post, we passed the ten-stamp quartz mill of the Apache Pass Mining Company, which, for want of water, was then lying idle.[39] It was about 10 o'clock in the forenoon when our ambulances drew up in front of the officers' quarters, and we were quartered as follows: Col. Stoneman and Major Cogswell, with Captain R. F. Barnard;[40] Doctor Wirtz and ourself, with Captain Gerald Russell[41] and Dr. W. H. Smith,[42] and we assure the reader that all fared sumptuously. During the afternoon, Dr. Smith piloted us around the post, and pointed out almost everything that was worth seeing. As the post trader's store of Tully, Ochoa, & Co.,[43] was the first institution met with, we entered it, expecting to get maimed or wounded, for we knew that Sydney R. DeLong, one of the firm, who had charge of it, had good reason for not loving us too well.[44] Now, most of our Territorial readers will recollect the fact that Mr. DeLong edited the Tucson *Arizonan* for a long time; that during that time, the *Arizonan* and *Miner* had several wordy encounters; that the Tucson paper generally got the best of us, and that's just what we expected would influence Mr. DeLong to "mash" us into pulp. But, luckily, he had gone a short distance from home, and we marched bodly through the premises and partook of the numerous good things offered us by his accommodating and generous assistants. The building — a large adobe — was scrupulously clean, and well filled with everything used by soldiers and citizens. In one room, was as fine a billiard table as any in the Territory, which had been brought all the way from St. Louis, Mo., at considerable cost. Having seen all the sights here, we started down hill. A few steps brought us to the springs, around which a portion of the California Column once had a brisk fight with Indians, for possession of the water. We believe the head of the column had reached within rifle shot of the water, when it received a volley of bullets and arrows from the Indian column — which was posted on the

hill-tops, behind rocks, under the famous chief Cheis. We do
not now recollect more about this fight than that several
Americans lost their lives in it, and the whole column was
stayed in its onward march until a few howitzers were brought
up, placed in position, and Lo, the accursed Indian, shelled
out of his fortifications.[45]

Leaving this spot, we soon arrived at the quartz-mill,
which presented a very poverty stricken appearance. There
being no covering over the machinery, stamps, dies, engine,
etc., were badly rusted, and the whole concern was fast becoming worthless. Instinct led us to the dump pile, where lay
about a ton of refuse ore, in pieces of which, our eyes detected
several "colors" and small pieces of gold. The ledge crops out
of a high mountain not far from the mill, and is, no doubt, a
good one. The country rock in the vicinity is limestone, but
the greater portion of the Chiricahua range is granite. We
were told that the owners of the mill intended to move it to
Bear creek — distant four miles — where there is plenty of
water the year round. In answer to questions asked a party
of Rio Grande Mexicans who were making adobes around
the mill, we were told that "colors" of gold had been found in
several places in the range; that south of Bowie, the mountain
was much higher and covered with large pine trees. "But,"
said they, *"Los Apaches mucho malo,"* which told the whole
story, that they were afraid to explore the mountains for
richer diggings.

The next thing that attracted our attention was the
graveyard, in which reposed the bodies of many persons who
had lost their lives in combats with the Apaches; those who
had been waylaid and murdered, and a few who had died of
disease. Knowing that persons now living have friends buried
there, it may be a source of consolation to them to know that
the graves of their departed friends at Camp Bowie, are
marked with slabs, and that green grass grows upon every
mound.

While the Indians of this vicinity are, and have been, the
worst on this continent, we must do them the justice to state

what has been told us by scores of white men; that they were friendly to Americans until an unlucky circumstance occurred at the fort. Some stock had been stolen, these Indians were accused of the theft, but stoutly denied having done it, and laid the blame upon another and different band. Their assertions were not believed by the officer in charge of the post, who soon after invited several leading Indians to a feast. The Indians went, and while sitting in a tent that had been placed at their disposal, a guard was placed over them, when all but one — Cheis — found themselves prisoners. Cheis saw the armed guard approaching, and divining what it all meant, quickly, drew his knife, cut his way through, and effected his escape. The remainder, among them a young brother of Cheis, were placed in the guard house. Cheis then gathered the tribe, told them all that had happened, and made them swear vengeance against all Americans. Then commenced that terrible war with the Chiricahuas that has desolated southeastern Arizona, and which, for aught we know, is still going on.[46] The Indians repaired to the stations of the Overland Mail Company, captured every white man they could find, took them to a hill overlooking Camp Bowie, where ropes were tied around their necks, one end of each rope being fastened to the pummel of a saddle, for the Indians were all mounted upon good horses. Cheis then informed the commanding officer that unless he released the Indians inside of a certain time, the white prisoners in his hands should suffer death. The officer did not see fit to do as Cheis desired, and at the expiration of the time and a signal from Cheis, the Indians started their horses on a run, the necks of the poor whites were broken, and their bodies dragged over sharp rocks. Such is the tale told by whites who were then, are yet, in the country. From that day to this, Cheis and his tribe have sought and found vengeance, and the numerous graves of white men scattered through the country show how successful they have been. Recently, it was said that Cheis wished to cease war, and it is our earnest hope that a peace with him has ere this been concluded. He is said to be the ablest, bravest, finest-looking Apache now living; is known and has made himself felt all over Northern Mexico, as well as Arizona. Our first and only night at Bowie was passed with pleasure and profit to ourself, and we presume our fellow-travelers passed it likewise. We visited the post trader's establishment— and bearded the lion of the tribe of DeLong in his den, but, instead of scalping us, he attempted to drown us with champagne — which, of course, he found impossible. In a word, Mr. DeLong treated us well, often and kindly, and we shall never again accuse him of having a hankering after Aztec Dictionaries. Having branched out considerably upon Bowie and its surroundings, nothing is now left for us to say, but that it is a pretty, healthy, comfortable post, in a fine grazing and farming country, and in the midst of a rich quartz region. When we were there, it was garrisoned as follows: Troop G, 1st Cavalry, Captain R. F. Barnard; K, 3d Cavalry, Captain Gerald Rusell. Lieutenant W. H. Winters, 1st Cavalry,[47] was Quartermaster, Lieutenants L. L. O'Conor, Kyle and Whiting were absent. Capt. Barnard, Lieutenants Winters and Cushing have distinguished themselves fighting Indians. O'Connor [*sic*] and Cushing were after the Reds when we were there. Capt. Russell had not been there long enough to kill any Apaches, but the wounds received in the late war, attest his bravery. The Post Surgeon, W. H. Smith, was formerly stationed at Camp Verde, in this country, and made many inquiries after his old friends there and in Prescott. It was at Bowie that we first heard the news of the downfall of Napoleon III, and great was our astonishment thereat.

Monday, September 19. Traveled through a splendid grazing country, over an excellent road, and encamped in Sulphur Spring valley, near the base of the Dragoon range of mountains, where we found considerable poor water. The grass in the bottoms was quite pointed, so much so that it entered a pair of canvass shoes we wore, and caused us to tread lightly while passing over it. On the high lands the grass was good and plenty. The valley is an extensive one, and will yet be settled. During the time of the great rush to the

Burro mines,[48] a couple of men concluded to establish a station on a knoll, near the water, and immediately set to work building stone houses, which were nearly completed, when a quarrel arose between them, and both left the place and their improvements. Distance made, about *twenty-five miles*.

Tuesday, September 20. Heavy rains having fallen upon the mountain ranges in the vicinity during the afternoon and night of Monday, the air was quite chilly when we awoke this morning, and we fancied ourselves away up in the great ranges of Northern Arizona. Learning that the mail coach for the east had arrived during the night, we sallied forth in quest of news, but learned nothing further than that Lieutenants Cushing and Bourke,[49] with their gallant command, were encamped near Dragoon Springs,[50] having just returned there from chasing Apaches. We passed, on the road, a large train of wagons, which were drawn by oxen, belonging to the enterprising firm of Tully & Ochoa, of Tucson. The train was in charge of Mr. Tully, and was on its way to Tucson, with goods which had been purchased in St. Louis, and shipped by rail to Carson, the western terminus of the Kansas Pacific. Arrived about noon, at the Upper Crossing of the San Pedro river,[51] where we rested until about three o'clock, when we traveled on about ten miles, and made a dry camp. Whole distance traveled, about *thirty-five miles*. The wash from the mountains on either side of the road passed over to-day consisted of granite and quartz, and we know of no better section of Southern Arizona in which to prospect for gold, silver, and other minerals.

While stopping at the crossing of the San Pedro, we learned that that river rises in Sonora, in what is known as the Watchuque Mountains,[52] and flows northward towards the Gila, of which it is a tributary. It is about two hundred miles in length, and upon it are some excellent valleys, which are now being settled and brought under cultivation. The water — of which there is an abundance for purposes of irrigation, etc., runs in a narrow channel nearly all the way from its source to its mouth. The country in which it rises, is said to be a delightful one, heavily timbered with pine, etc., and covered with good grass. The only timber met with on the lower portion of the river is mesquite and cottonwood, but these are quite plenty. The lower bottoms are thickly covered with sacaton grass; the hills adjoining, with gramma, so that besides being a good farming country, it is well adapted to stock-raising. The climate is hot, but not oppressively so. Frost seldom falls. The farmers, of which there are nearly one hundred, between the Upper Crossing and the mouth of the river, plant barley in December and corn in April and May. Rain descends during the summer months, and it rained a little when we were there.

Wednesday, September 21. Being now distant about 40 miles from Tucson, the temporary capital of our well-beloved Territory, our chief determined upon making the entire distance in one day, so we got an early start, and the road being good and the weather cool, made good time to the Cienega,[53] where we nooned. In going to the Cienega, we passed the place where the red-skins had recently captured a mail, and murdered those who accompanied it. Torn letters and papers were thickly strewn around; freshly made graves, at the heads and feet of which low adobe walls had been built, marked the places where rested the remains of our white brothers, who had been waylaid, and cruelly murdered by bloodthirsty savages. Yet, this was but a repetition of many such similar sights witnessed since striking the main road, and we traveled on, mooding over the dangers incident to a trip through Arizona. We soon reached a fine adobe house, near the crossing of the Cienega, which we found empty, the two men who formerly kept it, having been murdered by Apaches. The house was in a bad position for defense, and the Indians had but little trouble in killing its inmates, entering and plundering it. We had not remained long at this place when three men — an American and two Mexicans — arrived. They informed us that two freight trains — bound for the Burro mines — were coming on, close behind, and that it was their third day out from Tucson. This surprised us; we wondered what had kept them so long on the road, but, so soon as we saw the trains pass, the wonder was that they had made the trip in so short a time. The mules were not much bigger than donkeys, and so thin that daylight could almost be seen through them. They were driven by Mexican teamsters, and had, no doubt, forgotten all about the taste of grain. With them were several good-looking *senoritas*. Leaving our wagons and escort to come on slowly, the two ambulances — with their human freight — rolled over the road at a rapid pace, and we entered Tucson long before the sun went down. After leaving the Cienega, which is a very long strip of good land, with a fine stream flowing through it, the country passed over in going to Tucson would be a desert but for the good grass that grows upon it. Here, the cactus family reigns supreme, and there are thousands of thorns upon every square yard, wherever the grass has not "choked out" the *chollars* and *saguars* [*sic*].

As this was our first visit to Tucson, we will endeavor to give our impressions of it; the people who reside there, and the surrounding country. First, then, the town is situated on the Santa Cruz, a small river which rises near and takes its name from the town of Santa Cruz, in Sonora. The houses, of which there are about 400 — large and small — are constructed of adobes; that is, the walls are of that material. Timber being scarce in the vicinity, and lumber very dear, the people have had to use the material at hand for roofing purposes, so we found that most, if not all, the roofs in town were made as follows: Rafters, of stout cottonwood or mesquite poles, had, after having been stripped of bark, been placed in position, and covered with long slender poles — either willow or those round, cane-like "fibres" which are split out of the *saguar*. These are covered with a layer of hay, or straw, and over all is placed a thick coating of mud, which, in time becomes dry and hard, but scarcely ever sufficiently so to prevent heavy rain drops from beating down into it. These drops, in soaking through, mingle with the dirt, and descend upon the inmates, their furniture, clothing, etc., regardless of all consequences. Of course there are some roofs in Tucson capable of turning the heaviest rains, but our observation led us to believe that they were few in number. The dwellings of the poor are whitewashed on the inside; those of the rich are plastered and whitewashed, and, if memory serves us rightly, several of the latter are neatly papered and richly furnished.

THE STORES,

of which there are a great many, are well finished on the inside; the front walls of many stores on the principal streets are plastered and painted on the outside, so as to resemble brick and stone. Most of them are well filled with goods, which were arranged in a very tasty manner. But we saw no store in Tucson that for size, beauty and finish, excelled the brick establishments of Prescott.

OTHER PUBLIC PLACES.

Dr. Wirtz and ourself having expressed a desire to visit the priests, Catholic Church, Convent, Sisters' School, Mr. Peter R. Brady[54] kindly offered his services, and we sallied forth under his guidance. Arriving at the public square, we entered the dwelling of the only two priests in the Territory of Arizona, and were welcomed by Father Jovenceau.[55] We next visited the Sisters — seven in number — and after the usual introduction entered into conversation regarding their school, etc.[56] This was on Saturday, and as school was not in session, we did not see the 150 children and young ladies who, we were told, usually attended. We were shown through the school-room, which was large, clean, comfortable, and decently furnished; told how the sisters had arrived in Tucson, poor in purse but rich in purpose; how the good citizens had aided them to build, fit up and start their school, and left to judge for ourselves the success that had attended their efforts to bring up the young in the way they should go, which, we had before learned from others, was great. We

then entered the church, a plain, unpretending edifice, without as much as a chair or bench, and with nothing to relieve
the eye but the altar, and the usual paintings and pictures
seen in churches of this denomination. Here and there we
noticed devout women on their knees, imploring God,
through His Apostles and Angels, to forgive sins they had
been guilty of. The church is yet in an unfinished state, and
we learned that it would never have reached this state of
advancement, but for the skilled labor performed upon it by
Bishop Salpointe.[57]

Leaving the church, we visited the Court House, which,
we were informed cost the county $17,000. It is a large adobe
building, containing court-room, jail, and several offices. In
the jail, were incarcerated several criminals, one, a woman,
for the murder of her husband. Two men were also there,
charged with murder. The cells appeared strong and secure,
but Mr. Brady did not trust to them, and told us that he relied
more on the savage dogs which we saw running loose about
the yard — ready to tear to pieces any prisoner who might
escape from a cell. These dogs were raised in the yard, and
seemed to understand their business thoroughly. There is a
fine hospital in the place, and a splendid two-story flouring
mill belonging to Lee & Scott.[58] The saloons are a feature of
the town, although they are not numerous according to the
population. Those belonging to F. M. Hodges, C. O. Brown,
Levin & Brichta, are fitted up in splendid style, and the lager
beer at the latter place was excellent. We noticed the words
"ice cream saloon," on one building, and wondered how they
managed to make the article without ice. The last census gave
the place a population of 3,200, but we believe these figures to
be too great by three or four hundred.

THE PEOPLE.

The great majority of the people are Mexicans from New and
old Mexico — but we were told that the place contained quite
a number of people — descendants of Mexicans — who were

born and brought up on the soil of Arizona. The Americans —
of whom we saw quite a number — appeared to be busy, earnest men. One peculiarity about many of them was, that they
smoked cigaritos instead of pipes and cigars.

The complaint used to exist that the streets of Tucson
were filthy in the extreme, but we did not find them so, and
the reason we did not was readily accounted for by the fact
that a strong, well-organized chain-gang had been at work
upon them for some time past. The main street is very
crooked, and in walking or riding through it, one is frequently
compelled to go up and down steep hills, the lots having never
been leveled off. Upon entering the town, we had some misgivings as to the kind of reception that awaited us from a
people whom we had fought and denounced for several years
past, and who might be excused for treating us coolly. Yet, we
were welcomed and kindly treated by all, and shall hereafter
endeavor to repay the kindness bestowed upon us by Col. Lee
and lady, G. H. Oury and lady, C. H. Lord and lady, Peter R.
Brady and lady, Wm. S. Oury and lady, Gov. Safford, Hon.
Coles Bashford, Mr. Dooner, Mr. Wasson, and numerous
other ladies and gentlemen. Having seen most of the town,
Gov. Safford drove us out among the ranches, and the reader
may rest assured that we saw some fine ones, which have produced two crops a year every year of the past century. That of
John B. Allen[59] was said to be the best ranch on the Santa
Cruz. We were informed that vegetables, of all kinds, grow
and flourish the year round.

In addition to being the seat of government of the Territory of Arizona, and the county of Pima, Tucson possesses
other advantages, resources and institutions, besides those
already mentioned, which have made her the largest town in
the Territory, and which, should they remain, will contribute
to her further progress. For instance, tho [*sic*] depot for sup-
plying government posts in Southern Arizona, is, in the way
of rents, etc., worth ten or twelve thousand dollars per month
to the town, and the small garrison within her limits is, also,
of considerable aid to the people of the place. Then, she

drives a good trade with the citizens and soldiers of Southern Arizona; travelers going East and West over the Southern Overland route; also, with the people of Sonora, Mexico. Were it not that the place is unhealthy during the summer months; that it cannot much longer remain the seat of government of Arizona; that it is located in a hot climate, and in a country upon which the eyes of Heaven shed but few tears, we would have high hopes for its continuing — for years to come — the largest, most important city in Arizona. But, with Prescott, Phoenix, Wickenburg, Arizona City, Ehrenberg and other growing places in view, we cannot but think that Tucson will soon have to yield the palm. The city is now, however, a fixed fact, and if its citizens wish to accelerate its growth and prosperity, they have but to pay more attention to the development of the rich silver mines in the vicinity; and procure more water by means of artesian wells, to irrigate the large and fertile valleys of the Santa Cruz and other streams. Our next visit was to the noble pile — the ancient church of San Xavier — which stands near the southern bank of the Santa Cruz about 9 miles south from Tucson. The road wound through fine ranches, and tall mesquite trees, for about 8 miles, when it entered an open plain, and we got a view of the old church, which, at first, did not impress us as being anything grand. But, Dr. Wirtz and ourself were really astonished when we alighted and took a good view of the edifice — both inside and out. We regret, exceedingly, our inability to give a good description of it, but as that has already been done by J. Ross Browne and others, we shall content ourself with saying that it is of Moorish architecture, and large enough to accommodate a thousand or fifteen hundred persons. The walls are very high, and constructed of brick. The arched roof is of the same material, with the addition of a coating of cement, upon which the elements have made but little impression. The dome rises high above the building, and is a magnificent piece of workmanship, as are, also, the statues that adorn the outer walls, and which are of brick and plaster. The outer face of the front walls have a thick coating of plaster, which was beautified by inserting little black pebbles at suitable distances. Inside, the building presents a dazzling appearance, well calculated to impress the gazer with awe and admiration, and no doubt, its barbaric splendor has at time struck terror into the Indians who formerly worshipped there. Paintings, statues, pictures of winged angels, meet the eye in every direction. But the altar, and the ornamental work above, and upon two sides of it, are what astonishes the beholder. The paintings are not masterpieces, yet they are above an average. Some of the figures are perfect types of beauty. The floor is of cement — hard and dry — and far superior to any that can be made there at the present day. Service is occasionally held in the old church, for the benefit of the Papagoes and Mexicans living in the vicinity. The building is said to be about 100 years old, and to have been built by the hands of the Jesuit Fathers.[60] The wooden door leading to the vestry-room has the maker's name upon it, and the date 1797, but the church is much older than this door. The bells — of which there are several — bear no date; at least, we failed to discover any. Some of the figures on the outside are fast going to decay, as are, also, portions of the roof and walls. This decay ought to be stopped, and the grand old edifice preserved in all its splendor.

Sunday, September 25. General Stoneman and his brother officers having got through with their business, at Tucson, we started about three o'clock, on the afternoon of this day, made about *twenty* miles, and encamped near the base of the large mountain northeast of town. The country passed over was not such a one as we should desire to reside in. We saw no water, and but very little grass. Mesquite trees were plenty; so, also, were those ornaments of the desert — *chollars* and *saguars* — the latter the largest specimens of the genus we had ever seen, some of them having been upwards of thirty feet in height. But, the drive was a pleasant one, for it brought to view many curious sights, prominent among which was the "Picacho," a lone, queer looking peak which stands to the westward of Tucson, and can be seen for a long distance from the east, the west and the north. It was late in the night, when the order to camp was given. Animals were soon freed from their trammels, a sentinel was posted, when the whole party rolled into their blankets to sleep and rest. We, foolishly, threw away the mattrass [*sic*] which had been of so much service to us since our departure from Prescott, and, without sufficient covering, stretched ourself out in Col. Stoneman's ambulance, upon a camp-stool and two cushions. A stiff breeze soon came up from the south; we felt quite chilly, but laziness prevented us from reaching out after more blankets, and we arose, next morning, in a battered condition, from the pains which shot through our bones. We had contracted a bad cold, and a worse ague, which latter still sticks to us. But, we were not the only person that "caught it" on that night. Lieutenants Cushing and Bourke, two gallant young officers — came out from Tucson to see Colonel Stoneman about going after Cheis. The Colonel, Major Cogswell and Dr. Wirtz got out of their beds, and while the conversation was going on, Col. Stoneman got chilled "through and through," and, of course, acquired as good a title to ache and shake as that which we had, so that from that time on Major Cogswell, who took the ague at Camp Goodwin, had plenty of shaky assistants. From that night on, we suffered terribly, and but for Dr. Wirtz, all three of us would have "pegged out" on the hot desert.

Monday, September 26. We got a very early start, and soon rounded the point of the mountain, when the country changed for the better, it being more elevated. The difference between the north and south sides of the mountain was, indeed, great. On the south, it looked bare and barren. On the north, grass of good quality was plenty; trees were visible on the mountain, and along the bed of the *Canyon del Oro*,[61] a small stream which drains the mountains, and, it is said, contains gold in paying quantities. We stopped awhile to graze and water the animals, near the spot where a large party of Indians had, some time previous, attacked the train of Tully & Ochoa, killed several of the teamsters, captured most of the animals and robbed the wagons.[62] In all our rambles through the Territory, we have never seen a more suitable place for Indians to fight in their peculiar way. The formation being granite, ledges of that rock rise up at convenient distances for about two miles. These ledges are sufficiently high to hide Indians from persons ascending the hill, and if the red men were driven from behind one ledge, a few jumps would place them safely behind another, when they could fire upon their victims without danger to themselves. But a little while ago, at this place, a party of savages blazed away at Major Morrow, of the Pay Department, U.S. Army, while he was on his way to Camp Grant accompanied by Sylvester Mowry and a small escort of troops, and might have killed and captured the little party had it not been for the men of a train that was in camp close by. Men and animals having rested and refreshed themselves, we were soon again in motion, and moved slowly, up hill, past the graves of the men who had lost their lives in the fight we have spoken of. Our road led through an open, grassy country for about 20 miles, when it entered a very ugly cañon, with sandy bed, and precipitous walls.[63] While passing through this dangerous rent in the mountains, our eyes kept busy watch for Apaches, but none were there to interfere with our pasage, which was lucky for us, as ten Indians could prevent the passage of an entire company of men. We got through it at last, crossed the San Pedro and were soon in the garrison, where we met a cordial reception from the officers. Resting places were soon assigned us, a good supper indulged in, after which the evening was passed in discussing Military and Indian affairs, until we were admonished to retire to sleep.

Tuesday, September 27 was spent at Grant,[64] and a busy, hard day it was for Colonel Stoneman and Major Cogswell, who had lots of business to attend to, and who had suffered from sickness the previous night. Early in the morning, the troops assembled on the parade ground where they were closely inspected and put through various maneuvres by Major Cogswell. This being done, the work of inspecting quarters, Commissary and Quartermaster's stores began, and was not ended until late in the afternoon. While this was being done, we took a ride to the company gardens, on the San Pedro, and were shown through them by Captain Netterville.[65] They were the finest, best cultivated gardens we had seen in the Territory, and officers and men were justly proud of them. Tomatoes, onions, beets, cabbages, carrots, etc., were there in abundance, and of such size as to astonish those who beheld them, as well as to force upon them the knowledge that the soil of the San Pedro bottoms was extremely rich and fertile.

GRANT

stands upon high ground, in the delta formed by the San Pedro and Arivipa [*sic*] rivers. The houses are of adobe; the climate is hot and sickly. We believe the post was formerly known as "Buchanan."[66] It is in the heart of the Pinal-Apache country, and some effective scouts have been made from it by Captain Netterville and other officers. Pinal and Saddle Mountains, two noted landmarks, are within plain view of the post. When we were there, it was garrisoned by three small companies, and the following named officers —

Captain I. R. Dunkelberger, 1st Cavalry, Commanding Post. First Lieutenant John D. Hall, Assistant Surgeon, U.S.A., Post Surgeon. Captain W. McC. Netterville, 21st Infantry. First Lieutenant V. M. C. Silva, 21st Infantry. First Lieutenant T. F. Riley, 21st Infantry. First Lieutenant A. J. Garrett, 1st Cavalry. Second Lieutenant George R. Bacon, 1st Cavalry, A.A.Q.M., A.C.S., and Acting Post Adjutant. Acting Assistant Surgeon W. B. Dods. First Lieutenant H. B. Cushing, 3d Cavalry, and Second Lieutenant John G. Bourke, 3d Cavalry, were on detached service.

Wednesday, September 28. We got an early start from Grant, and were making good time up the cañon, when it was discovered that the teamsters had forgotten to draw forage for their animals. Word was sent back, and the necessary forage arrived in about an hour, when we bade adieu to Captain Netterville, and Lieutenants Riley and Garrett, who had accompanied us thus far. The hour was spent by Colonel Stoneman in talking with Captain Netterville about the new post which the Captain, with Lieutenants Silva and Barrett, Company "E," 21st Infantry, and "K" troop, 3d Cavalry, were about to start on Mineral Creek, near Pinal Mountain, and which is now established.[67] After going about 35 miles, over a country in which there was not a drop of water, but plenty of grass, we encamped late in the night, and slept a little while the animals were being fed. On the way, we passed two or three places where white men had been killed by savages, and saw the graves of the murdered men. Distance traveled, about 35 *miles.*

Thursday, September 29. We were up and away long before daylight and soon reached the Gila river, at Florence, when men and animals slaked their thirst, which was great, as we had made about 53 miles without water. The bottoms of the Gila, at this point, are large, and the soil very productive. Cottonwood and Mesquite were thick. Fine farms, and substantial adobe houses were seen on every side, and we could not help feeling pleased at once more beholding these evidences of civilization. Thomas R. Ewing,[68] who owns the finest ranch at this place, was very kind to us. He informed us that most of the river bottoms for 30 or 40 miles, were settled and under cultivation. The Gila furnishes plenty of water for purposes of irrigation, and the rule is to raise two crops a year. It was late in the afternoon when we started from Florence, and crossed the Gila, on our way to Camp McDowell. Twenty miles were soon passed, and we lay down on the desert to rest, having made, with our morning's journey of 18 miles, a distance of 38 *miles.*

Friday, September 30. Got an early start, and reached the Upper Crossing of Salt river about noon, crossed it and rested near a farmhouse. While approaching the river, we got a fine view of the immense valley in which stands the town of Phoenix, and in which are many of the finest ranches in Arizona. We had friends there whom we would have gone to see but for the fever and ague which was preying upon us. Salt River, or Rio Salado, as some call it, is, next to the Colorado, the largest stream that flows near or through Arizona. The water was low when our party crossed it, yet it was with some difficulty we made the trip. The wash, in its bed, and on its banks is made up, principally, of granite and quartz bowlders, which strengthened our belief that the stream passes through mineral bearing regions, above in Central Arizona. Three years ago there were not to exceed ten settlers upon this portion of the river; to-day, there are nearly 300, and the population is rapidly increasing. Scores of miles of ditches to convey water for irrigating, have been constructed, and the place is really the granary of Northern Arizona. Soon as the heat, which had been intense, became less, we took up the line of march for Camp McDowell, where we arrived about 8 o'clock in the evening.[69] On the march we passed some immense ruins. The road, from Salt river to McDowell, follows the west bank of the Verde, one of the largest and prettiest streams in the Territory, and upon which the post is located. Mesquite, *Palo Verde,* Cottonwood, and other trees were plenty in the vicinity, but grass was scarce, save on the river bottoms. The post itself is, we think, the finest in the Territory. The houses, of which there are a great number, are of adobe, well ventilated and scrupulously clean, as, indeed, was the large parade ground, and every place and thing in and about the post. It has, for a long time past, been commanded by that brave officer, Colonel G. B. Sanford,[70] who, with his noble troop, has inflicted many telling blows on the Apaches. The other officers of the post were Captain Moulton, Lieut. Veil C. De Witt, Surgeon, and Field Surgeon D. J. Evans. Troops — "C" and "E," 1st Cavalry, and "A," 21st Infantry. The sutler's store of W. B. Hellings & Co.[71] is the finest, best stocked establishment of the kind in the Territory, and its proprietors, Messrs. Hellings & Grubb, are gentlemen in every sense of the term.

The four peaks, which so many of our prospectors have

seen from a distance, are not far from McDowell, and though they look barren and forbidding, Colonel Sanford assured us that he had found pine timber, and water, in valleys, between the peaks. He and his troopers once surprised a rancheria up there, and killed several of its inmates.

The ranks of the two Cavalry companies were nearly full, and a finer lot of men are not to be found in the Territory. Captain Collins' Infantry company was very small, but every man in the company was a veteran. All the troops went through their drill in a very creditable manner. We missed seeing a Cavalry guard-mount, and were sorry for it, as Dr. Wirtz informed us that it was "splendidly done," by men and horses.

Saturday, October 1st. Since crossing the Upper Gila, we had traveled upon old and good roads, but now, we were about to take a new "road," over portions of which a vehicle of any sort had never passed. Therefore, we called upon Colonel Stoneman quite early, to learn the news. It was not very encouraging. He read us a letter from Colonel Frank Wheaton,[72] who had reconnoitered the route, and gave, in the letter, his opinion, that Colonel Stoneman would find it impossible to take his ambulances over the route. This fell on us "like a wet blanket." But, Stoneman said he would see whether or not he could make it. This suited us, as we were exceedingly anxious to get a breath of mountain air, and to see pine trees again. Our old and reliable escort, teamsters, wagons and teams, were ordered to turn back to Salt River, and take the road *via* Phoenix and Wickenburg, to Whipple, which they did. About 4 o'clock in the afternoon, the two ambulances were in readiness, we jumped in and followed a small escort. We made about ten miles that afternoon, through a poor-looking country, and camped for the night.

Sunday, October 2d. Made an early start; were, soon after starting, joined by Col. Sanford, Mr. Grubb, and some cavalrymen. Reached Cave creek[73] in about 10 miles travel; found plenty of wood, water and grass; rested a few hours, and put out again for next camp — New River[74] — distant

about ten miles, where we arrived late at night, very much
fatigued, for the road had been rough and hilly. We found
plenty of water in the stream, and refreshed ourselves.

Monday, October 3. Made about *ten miles* to-day, over
a rather rough road, and encamped on the east bank of the
Agua Frio, within plain view of the mouths of Black Cañon[75]
or Turkey creek, and the big, black cañon of the Agua Frio.
After dinner, Capt. Sanford, Mr. Grubb, and a few cavalrymen, started up the mountain to search for the men of Company F, 12th Infantry, who, we knew, were close by, building
a road. The Captain missed the men and their camp, in going
up the mountain, and kept on until he reached the Agua
Frio, where he got directions regarding their whereabouts.
He then returned, found them, and arrived in camp early
next morning, with the news, which was, if anything, more
discouraging than that contained in the letter of Col. Wheaton. But Stoneman had reconnoitered the mountain, the
previous evening, and knowing not the word fail, he gave
orders for the wagon to return to Camp McDowell; also, to
lighten up the ambulance as much as possible, and hitch up.
The ambulances were lightened and we started up Black
Canyon, over a rough road, which, however, was nothing in
comparison to what we afterwards encountered. When just
about ready to commence the ascent of the mountain, Sergeant John Powers, of E. Troop, First Cavalry, and one private, made their appearance. The Sergeant was on his return
to meet Colonel Stoneman, with an answer to a dispatch the
Colonel had sent Capt. Brown, commanding Camp Verde.
His story was short. He and his companion had ridden about
one hundred miles in fourteen hours, and lost one man on
the way, who became deranged, and rode off in search of
water. The Sergeant followed him, and found his horse,
which had been stripped of saddle and bridle. When he
found the man's horse thus stripped, he gave the man up for
lost, and started on. This occurred near the Agua Frio. We
afterwards found the man's saddle and bridle, and the man
himself, who said he had been chased by Indians, which was

all in his imagination. After thanking the Sergeant and his companion for the long, swift ride they had made, Stoneman led the way, and we started in climbing, and such climbing! Why, a California packer would not have attempted to drive his pack-train over such a mountain. But, it was the best we could do, and on we went, "slow like a snail," over great, rough trap bowlders, some of which were as large as an ambulance. Now and then, the animals had to be unhitched, and the ambulances pulled up by means of ropes. Oh! it was trying on nerves. Our poor nerves gave out early in the day, and leaving officers and men to "do their duty, nobly," we crawled to camp, where we found Lieutenant King, Dr. Soule, and other friends, who gave us something to eat and drink, and a good bed to shake in. It was about 5 o'clock in the afternoon, when we got over our shake and fever, and thinking our party ought to be near port, we started out to hail them, if in sight. They were in sight, and soon landed on the summit, tired and hungry, after their hard day's work — a day that had told fearfully on men and animals. Capt. Brown having arrived from Camp Verde, during the afternoon, with a pretty fair escort, Colonel Stoneman thanked Captain Sanford and his men for well performed services, and, in the kindest manner possible, ordered the Captain to turn back to his post. We then started on over a ten-mile mesa, that would have been level, but for the great number of hard-hearted nigger-head bowlders, which made the ride very unpleasant. We made a dry camp, and all, save the sentinels, slept as soundly as ever tired men slept.

Tuesday, October 4. We got up early, and having left the *trap* behind us, we traveled at a good gait over a nice granite road. Arriving at the Agua Frio, we stayed a few hours, hitched up again, and drive to Lerty's[76] place, where, we encamped all night. Distance traveled, about *twenty* miles. Mr. Lerty and Mrs. Branaman contributed liberally to our mess, and we had a glorious time eating pies and eggs, luxuries to which we had, for some time past, been strangers. Since leaving Black Cañon, the air had been quite chilly, which rather pleased us, after our long spell of suffering down south.

It was about ten o'clock, on the morning of the 5th of October, when we alighted at Colonel Stoneman's tent, near Fort Whipple and Prescott, and were welcomed back by Lieutenant E. W. Stone,[72] who appeared as glad to see us back safe, as we were to see him, and our own beautiful country, a country we would not trade for any we had seen in our ride of about 800 miles, through Arizona, notwithstanding that we had seen and passed through some beautiful regions.

In conclusion, we wish to state our belief, that no State or Territory on the Pacific slope offers greater inducements to labor and capital — than badly abused, illy treated, neglected Arizona, and that, as soon as both these needed elements shall have found their way within her borders, the progress she will then make; the wealth she will then contribute to the world, will be as great if not greater than California. But, croakers may say, "the day is far distant when the resources of Arizona shall have become available." We think not, for despite all the drawbacks from Indian wars, isolation, and partial failure to work mines, Arizona has progressed — is progressing. Possessing, as she does, vast forests of timber, an immense area of the best pastoral land in the world, a fair quantity of rich agricultural land, pure water, fine, healthy climate, rich and extensive mineral resources, and, last, but not least, the key to the Pacific — (for through her Territory are the only practicable routes for the great railroad that are soon to be built from the Atlantic and Gulf States to those of the Pacific) , we think — and the thought does not appear to be an extravigant [*sic*] one — that in less than ten years from to-day, Arizona will have sufficient wealth and population to entitle her to enter the Union as a full and equal partner.

NOTES

1. See Introduction.

2. Milton Cogswell of Indiana was a graduate of West Point. He served in the Civil War and was breveted colonel in 1861. He was promoted to major in 1869 and assigned to the 21st Infantry in March 1869. He retired in 1871, a year after his Arizona trip. Unless otherwise noted information on officers mentioned in this narrative is taken from Francis B. Heitman, *Historical Register and Dictionary of the United States Army.* . . .

3. Horace Raquet Wirtz arrived in Prescott with Stoneman July 3, 1870. He had served in the army over twenty-four years, crossed the continent over twelve times and had been shipwrecked twice, "escaped death repeatedly, and, to crown all, served at Fort Yuma a couple of years." *Miner*, Aug. 6, 1870.

4. Kimball was post trader at Camp Date Creek in 1870; he was later postmaster.

5. Through the kindness of Mr. James E. Serven of Tucson, Mr. Don H. Berkebile of the Division of Transportation, Smithsonian Institution, quotes the following from the *Harness & Carriage Journal* of 1871: "Sand Board — A broad piece of timber bolted to the top of the front hounds of a farm wagon and extending the full length of the axle between the hubs." Mr. Berkebile has provided me with a picture from Cray Brothers Cleveland, Ohio catalogue of wagon stock from 1910. It would appear that the Sand Board was placed parallel to and beneath the top bolster. The wagon experts in the Southwest with whom I have spoken do not know the term Sand Board, and thus its position and function still are not entirely clear.

6. James M. Baker was born in Missouri, went to California in 1853 and then wandered as far as Montana before coming to Prescott in 1866 according to a manuscript in the Bancroft Library. The *Miner* of April 10, 1869, says he arrived in Prescott with nearly one thousand California sheep.

7. George Washington Banghart, 1823-1895, was a Yavapai County pioneer who established a ranch about twenty-two miles northeast of Prescott. On August 27, 1870 the *Miner* reported he had one hundred fifty acres in corn and twelve acres of potatoes. His eldest daughter married Edmund W. Wells, October 5, 1869. His daughter Florence became Mrs. John H. Marion in September, 1873. See Introduction.

8. Trap is any of various dark, igneous rocks.

9. A deep canyon rising on the southwest slopes of Bill Williams Mountain and emptying into the Verde about five miles west of present Perkinsville. It was very rough. The name is said to date back to a military skirmish July 3, 1869. Unless otherwise noted geographical information is taken from Will C. Barnes *Arizona Place Names* and *Arizona Place Names,* 2nd Edition, revised and enlarged by Byrd H. Granger.

10. The present road leaves Prescott-Ashfork highway at Chino Valley and crosses the open valley, unfenced in places, looking today much as it must have in 1870, and finally turning northeast through the hills and descending to the Verde at the Perkins ranch (Perkinsville). From Perkinsville the road turns north climbing and winding among the foothills southeast of Bill Williams Mountain. It passes about a mile east of Bear Springs about nine miles south of Williams.

11. Above Fort Valley about seven miles from Flagstaff. A popular stopping place often mentioned in travel accounts. Named for the French guide and explorer Antoine Leroux. This beautiful area is still relatively unspoiled.

12. Spring at which Beale camped in 1858 about four miles south of San Francisco Spring. Early maps locate the spring southeast of the peaks. Marion's narrative is not easy to follow here. It gives the impression that the party traveled along the west side and around the north of the peaks, but the established trail went south of the peaks, more or less in line with present Highway 66, or Interstate 40.

13. Probably Sunset Crater.

14. Situated eleven miles east of Flagstaff on the Walnut Creek drainage about ten miles downstream towards the Little Colorado from Walnut Canyon National Monument. Named for the Cosnino tribe supposed to have lived there. Also referred to as the Turkey Tanks caves. Information from Katharine Bartlett of Flagstaff.

15. Same as the present Canyon Diablo about twenty-six miles west of Winslow. Crossed by the Santa Fe railroad and Highway 66, or, new Interstate 40.

16. Early and frequently mentioned ford of the Little Colorado at the site of a rock ledge that formed the bed of the river from bank to bank about six miles east of present Winslow. Martha Summerhayes describes ambulances being ferried here in Chapter Fifteen of her book *Vanished Arizona.*

17. Frank Kidder Upham, a veteran of the Civil War from Maine, had been promoted to permanent rank of first lieutenant in August, 1869.

18. See note 23.

19. Uncertain, possibly Leroux Wash.

20. The Army Chief of Engineers map of 1879 locates Leroux Crossing just east of the present town of Holbrook.

21. Granger says the name is now synonymous with old Big Dry Wash. The route is not entirely clear here; however, the stream the Stoneman party followed is probably Silver Creek which flows from the Fort Apache Indian Reservation north past Snowflake and into the Little Colorado about four miles south of Woodruff. It is the only perennial stream in the area. Martha Summerhayes, retracing the route in 1875, says the party followed Silver Creek.

22. The White River, so called because the waters come from the White Mountains, is formed at Fort Apache by the junction of the North Fork and the East Fork.

23. The site which Marion describes was established May 16, 1870, as Camp Ord. The name was changed to Camp Mogollon, for the mountains, on July 1. On September 12, it was named Camp Thomas. It was visited by Cochise in late summer, and February 2, 1871, it was changed to Camp Apache as a token of friendship. See Barnes, and Brandes, p. 10.

24. See *Miner*, January 26, 1867.

25. Charles Warren Foster, a native of New England, had been in the army since 1846 and had been breveted lieutenant colonel and colonel in the Civil War.

26. John Green was born in Germany in 1825. He entered the army from Ohio as a sergeant, became an officer during the Civil War and was made major, First Cavalry, 9 June, 1868. He was later awarded the Medal of Honor for bravery in the Modoc wars.

27. Like brother officers on the western frontier, most of these men were veterans of the Civil War who stayed on in army service.

28. Crook visited Apache in 1871. Of this visit Bourke writes that at "this lovely site lived a large number of the Apaches, under chiefs who were peaceably disposed towards the whites — men like the old Miguel, Eskitistsla, Pedro, Pitone, Alchise, and others, who expressed themselves as friendly, and showed by their actions the sincerity of their avowals. . . . Colonel John Green, of the First Cavalry, was in command, with two troops of his own regiment and two companies of the Twenty-third Infantry. Good feeling existed between the military and the Indians, and the latter seemed anxious to put themselves in 'the white man's road.' " Bourke p. 142.

29. This is the location of Fort Apache today.

30. Mowry, a native of Rhode Island, was one of Arizona's famous early pioneers. A graduate of West Point, he saw service at Fort Yuma in 1855. He was deeply involved in urging early recognition of Arizona as a Territory. He was owner of the famous Mowry Mine and author of the *Memoir on the Proposed Territory of Arizona* and *Arizona and Sonora*, an early promotional work. He has been described as genial and dashing. Unfortunately he chose the wrong side in the Civil War, was arrested, stripped of his properties, and though later released, he never recouped his fortunes.

He died in London in 1871, not yet forty years of age. For further details the reader is referred to Frank C. Lockwood's *Life in Old Tucson* and B. Sacks' "Sylvester Mowry" in *The American West*, vol. 1, pp. 14-24, Summer 1964.

31. The Black River and the Natanes Plateau?

32. Established June, 1864. Its location near the Gila, on a stream King Woolsey said was the Tularosa, was notoriously unhealthy. Named in honor of the first governor of Arizona. Writing of his visit in 1866 Marion said, "The soldiers do scarcely any scouting. They are principally engaged in making adobes and escorting trains of provisions for the Coyotero Apaches." *Miner*, Jan. 26, 1867.

33. Henry Englers Lacy, 1828–1900, born in England and came to the United States in 1864. He was with the California Volunteers at Goodwin in 1865, and after his discharge in 1866 returned as post trader until the camp was disbanded in 1871. He was later at Apache until 1884. Ms. in the Bancroft Library.

34. Pueblo Viejo, in Graham County. A Mexican hamlet about two miles southeast of Safford, named from pre-Columbian ruins in the vicinity.

35. A few survivors of this forest, still fairly extensive fifteen years ago, can be seen along the Nogales highway south of the present Tucson airport. There are still a few mesquite groves near Tucson, the best, perhaps, on the Tanque Verde road en route to Mt. Lemmon.

36. On the headwaters of the Gila in New Mexico.

37. The narrow defile between the Chiricahua and Dos Cabezas Mountains. The scene of much Apache fighting. There were springs here, and a station of the Butterfield Stage was established there in 1857.

38. Camp Bowie was established in Apache Pass on July 28, 1862, following the famous Battle of Apache Pass between Carleton's Column and the Indians, in June of 1862. It was the scene of much activity until the final defeat of the Apaches in 1886.

39. J. B. Tenney in his manuscript history of mining in Arizona, now in the Special Collections division of the University of Arizona Library, says the mines were probably located before the Civil War. They may have been reopened in 1867, but the July 10 *Arizonian* says the company was without capital or organization. There was some activity in 1870, but the mines were abandoned following the murder of John F. Stone, the superintendent. See also *Arizona Historical Review*, vol. 6, July, 1935, pp. 74–80.

40. Reuben Frank Bernard of Tennessee who entered the army as a private in 1855, had a distinguished record during the Civil War. In 1890 he was breveted brigadier general for, among other things, gallant service against the Indians at "Chiricahua Pass."

41. Gerald Russell, born in Ireland, had served in the army since 1851, rising from the rank of private. He was breveted first lieutenant for gallantry at the siege of Vicksburg.

42. William H. Smith, a contract surgeon, had been at Camp Verde from January to May, 1869 and served at Bowie until February, 1871. In July the *Citizen* reported he had left for the East. The census of 1870 lists a W. H. Smith, age twenty-seven born in Canada, from Apache Pass, presumably the doctor. Information from Frances Quebbeman.

43. Pinckney Randolph Tully, a native of Mississippi, and Estevan Ochoa, a native of Chihuahua, formed a partnership in 1863 or 1864 according to Lockwood. They were for many years among the most prominent and successful freighters and merchandisers in the Southwest. In the *Citizen* October 15, 1870, they advertise that at their store at Bowie they have a complete stock of dry goods, clothing, boots and shoes, groceries and provisions, and miners' tools "which we offer at the lowest rates."

44. Sidney Randolph DeLong was born in Clinton County, N. Y., Dec. 28, 1828 and died in Tucson in 1914. He sailed around the Horn to California in 1849. He first came to Arizona with the California Column and after being mustered out at Santa Fe in 1866 returned to Tucson. He was at this time associated with Tully and Ochoa. He was a trader, miner, mayor of Tucson in 1872, and legislator. Marion refers here to the time when he and DeLong had crossed journalistic swords during the latter's brief editorship of the *Arizonian* in 1867.

45. The Battle of Apache Pass, July 15, 1862. A vivid first-hand account is given in John C. Cremony's *Life among the Apaches.*

46. A somewhat inaccurate version of the notorious Bascom affair of 1860. For a good, brief account see Lockwood's *Pioneer Days in Arizona.* N. Y., Macmillan, 1932.

47. Also veterans of the Civil War, experienced officers who formed the backbone of the officer corps in the West.

48. Silver discoveries at the Burro Mines caused great excitement in Tucson in late 1870. The *Arizonian* and the *Citizen* are full of speculation and stories of comings and goings. In spite of the claims of the *Arizonian* the mines were well inside the New Mexico boundary, not far from present Lordsburg.

49. Howard B. Cushing, a gallant and able officer, was killed by the Chiricahuas on May 5, 1871. Bourke pays him warm tribute in *On the Border with Crook*, pages 29–30 and 105. John Gregory Bourke, soldier, aide to General Crook, writer, ethnologist, was then a new lieutenant on the frontier. He was born in 1846 and graduated from West Point in 1869. He served fourteen years under Crook at posts in the West. As a writer he had a vivid and amusing style, and his *On the Border with Crook* is one of the classics of southwestern and western history.

50. In Dragoon Pass between Willcox and Benson. "It was at a well known spring in this pass that Gen. O. O. Howard, Oct. 12, 1872, ratified a treaty of peace with Cochise." Barnes, p. 124.

51. South of present Benson in the vicinity of St. David.

52. i.e. Huachuca Mountains.

53. In the pass between the San Pedro and Santa Cruz valleys. It is now bypassed by the highway, and the name seems likely to pass into oblivion.

54. Peter Rainsford Brady, born Washington, D. C., August 4, 1825, educated at Georgetown College, served in the Texas Rangers in the Mexican War. He was one of the organizers of the first company to operate the mines at Ajo in 1854 after accompanying A. B. Gray's Pacific railway survey. He was three times sheriff of Pima County and in 1870 was Democratic nominee to Congress. His early reminiscences have ben published recently in *The A. B. Gray Report.* Los Angeles, Westernlore Press, 1963.

55. Francis Xavier Jouvenceau came to Arizona as a missionary in 1866. He was parish priest during the absence of the Reverend J. B. Salpointe. See note 57.

56. The Sisters of St. Joseph had arrived in Tucson in May of 1870 to open the school which had been built for them near the church.

57. John Baptiste Salpointe, born in Clermont, France. Responding to a call for volunteers, he reached Arizona in 1866. He was made a bishop in 1868, and later he succeeded Lamy as archbishop of Santa Fe. He has left a record of his work in *Soldiers of the Cross.*

58. James Lee and William Fisher Scott, who already operated a mill on the Santa Cruz near Silver Lake, had just completed their new steam mill on the south side of the town. According to the *Arizonian* of August 6, one of the largest and most expensive buildings in Tucson.

59. John Brackett ("Pie") Allen, came to Arizona in 1857 and to Tucson in 1858. He was a business man, legislator, rancher, and twice mayor of Tucson. According to the *Arizonian* of April 4, 1869, his ranch was about two miles from Tucson. It had a large adobe corral which contained agricultural implements, wagons and mules. A house, sixty by forty feet, was being built and Brady was experimenting with various grain and vegetable crops.

60. Marion, of course, is in error here. San Xavier was built by the Franciscans. It is fairly certain construction began about 1783, and was completed by 1797. The Jesuits were expelled in 1767.

61. Canyon and stream flowing from the north slope of the Catalina Mountains and emptying into the Santa Cruz a few miles above Tucson. The old road to Camp Grant ran through the canyon which was the scene of a number of Apache ambushes.

62. This had occurred May 10, 1869. Lockwood estimated the company lost about $12,000 in the disaster.

63. Putnam Wash descends through a canyon and empties into the San Pedro oposite the site of Grant. No particular name is given the canyon on maps.

64. Grant, scene of the notorious Camp Grant Massacre of 1871, was established near the junction of the Aravaipa and the San Pedro in 1860. It was in an unhealthy location, and Bourke described it as "the most thoroughly godforsaken post of all those supposed to be included in the annual Congressional appropriations." He has other unkind things to say of it.

65. William McClellan Netterville, a native of New York, rose from private to brevet captain for gallant service in the Battle of the Wilderness during the Civil War.

66. Marion was wrong. Buchanan was southeast of Tucson near the Sonoita Creek between the present towns of Sonoita and Patagonia.

67. Grant was moved to its present location on the west side of Mt. Graham in 1872. Finally abandoned in 1895, its buildings were later turned over to the state for an industrial school.

68. Thomas R. Ewing was Florence's first postmaster having been appointed in August of 1869.

69. Established September 7, 1865, on the west bank of the Verde, seven miles above its junction with the Salt. It was a base of operations against the Tontos. Billings notes that in 1869 it had a library of three hundred books, mostly novels.

70. George Bliss Sanford, a native of Connecticut, had been breveted lieutenant colonel in March, 1865 for gallant and meritorious service. He served at various Arizona posts from the close of the war until 1890.

71. William B. Hellings was a well-known pioneer trader. In 1871, he began operation of one of the first two flour mills in the Salt River Valley at the site of the present state hospital at Twenty Fourth Street and Van Buren in Phoenix.

72. Frank Wheaton, a native of Rhode Island rose to the brevet rank of brigadier general in the Civil War. He ended his career in 1897 with the rank of major general.

73. Cave Creek rises in the Lime Creek Mountains and flows southeast to the Salt River Valley. Granger cites Marion as an early user of the name.

74. New River rises in Yavapai County and flows generally south to join the Agua Fria in the Salt River Valley. Presently also a small community on the Black Canyon highway (Highway 89) about thirty miles north of Phoenix.

75. Canyon on the east slopes of the Bradshaw Mountains roughly between the community of Bumble Bee and the junction with the Agua Fria. The road was just being developed and apparently Stoneman was the first to push a four-wheeled vehicle up what became the Black Canyon highway. The present highway is cut through the sides of the canyon, and from a lookout point, traces of the old road are clearly visible.

76. M. K. Lerty was a pioneer Yavapai rancher. "The place to stop at," says the *Miner* of 1868. "Persons who have occasion to travel over the road from Prescott to the Verde . . . and Black Canyon will consult their interest by stopping at the ranch of M. K. Lerty on Lynx Creek . . . . His latchstring hangs out, day and night, and he is prepared to put fat on the ribs of man and beast." Undated clipping in the Sharlot Hall Museum, Prescott.

77. Ebenezer Whitten Stone, a native of Massachusetts, had been breveted lieutenant and captain, then major, and finally lieutenant colonel for gallant service during battles of the Civil War. According to Heitman he was then unassigned, but was shortly assigned to the Twenty-First Infantry. He retired with the rank of major.

SELECTED BIBLIOGRAPHY

The following is a list of those books which I have consulted fairly often in preparing this edition of the text. It is not intended to be complete. Such lengthy listings, frequently found in editions like this, display a certain squirrel-like industry, but are relatively useless to the reader. In addition I have consulted manuscript and clipping files in the libraries of the University of Arizona, the Pioneers' Historical Society and Sharlot Hall Museum in Prescott. I am indebted, too, to many friends and colleagues who have listened to my chatter, who have made suggestions, and who have aided me above and beyond the call but who can in no way be responsible for my mistakes.

Barnes, Will C. *Arizona Place Names.* Tucson: University of Arizona, 1935. (University of Arizona General Bulletin no. 2)

Bourke, John G. *On the Border with Crook.* Columbus, Ohio: Long's College Book Co., 1950. A reprint of the 1897 edition.

Brandes, Ray. *Frontier Military Posts of Arizona.* Globe: Dale Stuart King, 1960.

Conner, Daniel E. *Joseph Reddeford Walker and the Arizona Adventure.* Edited by Donald J. Berthrong and Odessa Davenport. Norman: University of Oklahoma, 1956.

Granger, Byrd H. *Will C. Barnes' Arizona Place Names.* Revised and enlarged. Tucson: University of Arizona Press, 1960.

Heitman, Francis B. *Historical Register and Dictionary of the United States Army* . . . . Washington: Government Printing Office, 1903.

Hinton, Richard J. *The Hand-Book to Arizona.* Tucson: Arizona Silhouettes, 1954. Reprint of the 1878 edition.

Lockwood, Francis C. *Life in Old Tucson, 1854–1864.* Los Angeles: Ward Ritchie Press, 1943.

Lutrell, Estelle. *Newspapers and Periodicals of Arizona, 1859–1911.* Tucson: University of Arizona, 1950. (General Bulletin no. 15)

Salpointe, John B. *Soldiers of the Cross.* Banning, Calif.: St. Boniface's School, 1898.

Summerhayes, Martha. *Vanished Arizona.* Tucson: Arizona Silhouettes, 1960. Reprint of the second edition of 1911.

U.S. War Dept. Surgeon General's Office. *A Report on Barracks and Hospitals, with Descriptions of Military Posts.* By John S. Billings. Washington: Government Printing Office, 1870.

Weekly Arizona Miner, Prescott

Arizona Citizen, Tucson

Weekly Arizonan, Tucson

DONALD MOORE POWELL is a native New Yorker, graduate of New York schools, and of Swarthmore College. He received the degree of Master of Arts in English from Duke University and of Bachelor of Arts in Library Science from the University of Michigan. An employe of the New York Public Library, he interrupted his career to serve three years with the U.S. Army in North Africa, Italy, France, and Germany during World War Two.

Mr. Powell came to Tucson in 1946 as reference librarian of the University of Arizona and has been here since that time, except when he was consultant to the library of the Iraq College of Agriculture in 1957. He later became Chief of Public Services of the Library here, and in 1965 was appointed Assistant Librarian. His other publications include three books: THE PERALTA GRANT (University of Oklahoma Press, 1960), AN ARIZONA GATHERING (Arizona Pioneers' Historical Society, 1960) and ARIZONA FIFTY (published as a keepsake for the Arizona History Conference, 1962), and several articles on history and librarianship in professional journals.

The typeface in NOTES ON MARION'S TRAVELS is the Linotype form of Baskerville, designed by an English writing master who approached typography from the point of view of calligraphy. The modern version of the font, while varying slightly, maintains the characteristic sharpness and delicacy of the 18th-century original. The entire book was typeset and composed by the Tucson Typographic Service and printed by Arizona Lithographers on 70-pound Warren No. 66 textstock. The binding is Kivar No. 5, Sahara Kidskin. Erwin Acuntius is the designer.